Alexander Johnston

Representative american Orations

To illustrate american political History

Alexander Johnston

Representative american Orations
To illustrate american political History

ISBN/EAN: 9783337079017

Printed in Europe, USA, Canada, Australia, Japan

Cover: Foto ©ninafisch / pixelio.de

More available books at **www.hansebooks.com**

REPRESENTATIVE
AMERICAN ORATIONS

TO ILLUSTRATE
AMERICAN POLITICAL HISTORY

EDITED, WITH INTRODUCTIONS

BY

ALEXANDER JOHNSTON
PROFESSOR OF JURISPRUDENCE AND POLITICAL ECONOMY IN THE
COLLEGE OF NEW JERSEY

NEW YORK & LONDON
G. P. PUTNAM'S SONS
The Knickerbocker Press
1888

CONTENTS.

V.—THE ANTI-SLAVERY STRUGGLE.

	PAGE
THE ANTI-SLAVERY STRUGGLE	3
WENDELL PHILLIPS	33
On the Murder of Lovejoy; Faneuil Hall, Boston, December 8, 1837.	
JOHN C. CALHOUN	46
On the Slavery Question; Senate, March 4, 1850.	
DANIEL WEBSTER	84
On the Constitution and the Union; Senate of the United States, March 7, 1850.	
HENRY CLAY	118
On the Compromise of 1850; United States Senate, July 22, 1850.	
WENDELL PHILLIPS	135
On the Philosophy of the Abolition Movement, before the Massachusetts Anti-Slavery Society, at Boston, January 27, 1853.	
SALMON PORTLAND CHASE	183
On the Kansas-Nebraska Bill; Senate, February 3, 1854.	
CHARLES SUMNER	212
On the Kansas-Nebraska Bill; Senate, May 25, 1854.	
STEPHEN ARNOLD DOUGLAS	218
On the Kansas-Nebraska Bill; Senate, March 3, 1854.	
CHARLES SUMNER	256
On the Crime against Kansas; Senate, May 19-20, 1856.	

PRESTON S. BROOKS 289
    ON THE SUMNER ASSAULT; HOUSE OF REPRESENTATIVES,
    JULY 14, 1856.

ANSON BURLINGAME 297
    IN DEFENCE OF MASSACHUSETTS; HOUSE OF REPRESENTA-
    TIVES, JUNE 21, 1856.

THOMAS L. CLINGMAN 307
    ON "DEBATES" IN CONGRESS; HOUSE OF REPRESENTATIVES,
    JULY 9, 1856.

V.

ANTI-SLAVERY STRUGGLE.

V.

THE ANTI-SLAVERY STRUGGLE.

Negro slavery was introduced into all the English colonies of North America as a custom, and not under any warrant of law. The enslavement of the negro race was simply a matter against which no white person chose to enter a protest, or make resistance, while the negroes themselves were powerless to resist or even protest. In due course of time laws were passed by the Colonial Assemblies to protect property in negroes, while the home government, to the very last, actively protected and encouraged the slave trade to the colonies. Negro slavery in all the colonies had thus passed from custom to law before the American Revolution broke out; and the course of the Revolution itself had little or no effect on the system.

From the beginning, it was evident that the course of slavery in the two sections, North and South, was to be altogether divergent. In the colder North, the dominant race found it easier to work than to compel negroes to work: in the warmer South, the case was exactly reversed. At the close of the Revolution, Massachusetts led the way in an abolition of slavery, which was followed gradually by the other States north of Virginia; and in 1787 the ordinance of Congress organizing the Northwest Territory made all the future States north of the Ohio free States. "Mason and Dixon's line" and the Ohio River thus seemed, in 1790, to be the natural boundary between the free and the slave States.

Up to this point the white race in the two sections had dealt with slavery by methods which were simply divergent, not antagonistic. It was true that the percentage of slaves in the total population had been very rapidly decreasing in the North and not in the South, and that the gradual abolition of slavery was proceeding in the North alone, and that with increasing rapidity. But there was no positive evidence that the South was bulwarked in favor of slavery; there was no certainty but that the South would in its turn and in due time come to the point which the North had already reached, and begin its own abolition of slavery. The language of Washington, Jefferson, Madison, Henry, and Mason, in regard to the evils or the wickedness of the system of slavery, was too strong to be heard with patience in the South of after years; and in this section it seems to have been true, that those who thought at all upon the subject hoped sincerely for the gradual abolition of slavery in the South. The hope, indeed, was rather a sentiment than a purpose, but there seems to have been no good reason, before 1793, why the sentiment should not finally develop into a purpose.

All this was permanently changed, and the slavery policy of the South was made antagonistic to, and not merely divergent from, that of the North, by the invention of Whitney's saw gin for cleansing cotton in 1793. It had been known, before that year, that cotton could be cultivated in the South, but its cultivation was made unprofitable, and checked by the labor required to separate the seeds from the cotton. Whitney's invention increased the efficiency of this labor hundreds of times, and it became evident at once that the South enjoyed a practical monopoly of the production of cotton. The effect on the slavery policy of the South was immediate and unhappy. Since 1865, it has been found that the cotton monopoly of the South is even more complete under a free than under a slave labor system, but mere theory could never have convinced the Southern people that such would be the case. Their whole prosperity hinged on one product; they began its cultivation under slave labor; and the belief that labor and prosperity were equally dependent on the enslavement of the laboring race very soon made the dominant race active defenders of slavery. From that time the system in the South was one of slowly but steadily increasing rigor, until, just before 1860, its last development took the form of legal enactments for the re-enslavement of free negroes, in default of their leaving the State in which they resided. Parallel with this increase of rigor, there was a steady change in the character of the system. It tended very steadily to lose its original patriarchal character, and take the aspect of a purely commercial speculation. After 1850, the commercial aspect began to be the rule in the black belt of the Gulf States. The plantation knew only the overseer; so many slaves died to so many bales of cotton; and the slave population began to lose all human connection with the dominant race.

The acquisition of Louisiana in 1803 more than doubled the area of the United States, and far more than doubled the area of the slave system. Slavery had been introduced into Louisiana, as usual, by custom, and had then been sanctioned by Spanish and French law. It is true that Congress did not forbid slavery in the new territory of Louisiana; but Congress did even worse than this; under the guise of forbidding the importation of slaves into Louisiana, by the act of March 26, 1804, organizing the territory, the phrase "except by a citizen of the United States, removing into said territory for actual settlement, and being at the time of such removal *bona fide* owner of such slave or slaves," impliedly legitimated the domestic slave trade to Louisiana, and legalized slavery wherever population should extend between the Mississippi and the Rocky Mountains. The Congress of 1803–05, which passed the act, should rightfully bear the responsibility for all the subsequent growth of slavery, and for all the difficulties in which it involved the South and the country.

There were but two centres of population in Louisiana, New Orleans and St. Louis. When the southern district, around New Orleans, applied for admission as the slave State of Louisiana, there seems to have been no surprise or opposition on this score; the Federalist opposition to the admission is exactly represented by Quincy's speech in the first volume. When the northern district, around St. Louis, applied for admission as the slave State of Missouri, the inevitable consequences of the act of 1804 became evident for the first time, and all the Northern States united to resist the admission. The North controlled the House of Representatives, and the South the Senate; and, after a severe parliamentary struggle, the two bodies united in the compromise of 1820. By its terms Missouri was admitted as a slave State, and slavery was forever forbidden in the rest of Louisiana Territory, north of latitude 36° 30′ (the line of the southerly boundary of Missouri). The instinct of this first struggle against slavery extension seems to have been much the same as that of 1846–60—the realization that a permission to introduce slavery by custom into the Territories meant the formation of slave States exclusively, the restriction of the free States to the district between the Mississippi and the Atlantic, and the final conversion of the mass of the United States to a policy of enslavement of labor. But, on the surface, it was so entirely a struggle for the balance of power between the two sections, that it has not seemed worth while to introduce any of the few reported speeches of the time. The topic is more fully and fairly discussed in the subsequent debates on the Kansas-Nebraska Act.

In 1830 William Lloyd Garrison, a Boston printer, opened the real anti-slavery struggle. Up to this time the anti-slavery sentiment, North and South, had been content with the notion of "gradual abolition," with the hope that the South would, in some yet unsuspected manner, be brought to the Northern policy. This had been supplemented, to some extent, by the colonization society for colonizing negroes on the west coast of Africa, which had two aspects: at the South it was the means of ridding the country of the free negro population; at the North it was a means of mitigating, perhaps of gradually abolishing, slavery. Garrison, through his newspaper, the *Liberator*, called for "immediate abolition" of slavery, for the conversion of anti-slavery sentiment into anti-slavery purpose. This was followed by the organization of his adherents into the American Anti-Slavery Society in 1833, and the active dissemination of the immediate abolition principle by tracts, newspapers, and lecturers.

The anti-slavery struggle thus begun, never ceased until, in 1865, the *Liberator* ceased to be published, with the final abolition of slavery. In its inception and in all its development the movement was a distinct product of the democratic spirit. It would not have been possible in 1790, or in 1810, or in 1820. The man came with the hour; and every new mile of railroad or telegraph, every new district open to population, every new influence toward the growth of democracy, broadened the power as well as the field of the abolition movement. It was but the deepening, the application to an enslaved race of laborers, of the work which Jeffersonian democracy had done, to remove the infinitely less grievous restraints upon the white laborer thirty year before. It could never have been begun until individualism at the North had advanced so far that there was a reserve force of mind ready to reject all the influences of heredity and custom upon thought. Outside of religion there was no force so strong at the North as the reverence for the Constitution; it was significant of the growth of individualism, as well as of the anti-slavery sentiment, that Garrison could safely begin his work with the declaration that the Constitution itself was "a league with death and a covenant with hell."

The Garrisonian programme would undoubtedly have been considered highly objectionable by the South, even under the comparatively colorless slavery policy of 1790. Under the conditions to which cotton culture had advanced in 1830, it seemed to the South nothing less than a proposal to destroy, root and branch, the whole industry of that section, and it was received with corresponding indignation. Garrisonian abolitionists were taken and regarded as public enemies, and rewards were even offered for their capture. The germ of abolitionism in the Border States found a new and aggressive public sentiment arrayed against it; and an attempt to introduce gradual abolition in Virginia in 1832–33 was hopelessly defeated. The new question was even carried into Congress. A bill to prohibit the transportation of abolition documents by the Post-Office department was introduced, taken far enough to put leading men of both parties on the record, and then dropped. Petitions for the abolition of slavery in the District of Columbia were met by rules requiring the reference of such petitions without reading or action; but this only increased the number of petitions, by providing a new grievance to be petitioned against, and in 1842 the "gag rule" was rescinded. Thenceforth the pro-slavery members of Congress could do nothing, and could only become more exasperated under a system of passive resistance.

Even at the North, indifferent or politically hostile as it had hitherto shown itself to the expansion of slavery, the new doctrines were received with an outburst of anger which seems to have been primarily a revulsion against their unheard of individualism. If nothing, which had been the object of unquestioning popular reverence, from the Constitution down or up to the church organizations, was to be sacred against the criticism of the Garrisonians, it was certain that the innovators must submit for a time to a general proscription. Thus the Garrisonians were ostracised socially, and became the Ishmaelites of politics. Their meetings were broken up by mobs, their halls were destroyed, their schools were attacked by all the machinery of society and legislation, their printing presses were silenced by force or fraud, and their lecturers came to feel that they had not done their work with efficiency if a meeting passed without the throwing of stones or eggs at the building or the orators. It was, of course, inevitable that such a process should bring strong minds to the aid of the Garrisonians, at first from sympathy with persecuted individualism, and finally from sympathy with the cause itself; and in this way Garrisonianism was in a great measure relieved from open mob violence about 1840, though it never escaped it altogether until abolition meetings ceased to be necessary. One of the first and greatest reinforcements was the appearance of Wendell Phillips, whose speech at Faneuil Hall in 1837 was one of the first tokens of a serious break in the hitherto almost unanimous public opinion against Garrisonianism. Lovejoy, a Western anti-slavery preacher and editor, who had been driven from one place to another in Missouri and Illinois, had finally settled at Alton, and was there shot to death while defending his printing press against a mob. At a public meeting in Faneuil Hall, the Attorney-General of Massachusetts, James T. Austin, expressing what was doubtless the general sentiment of the time as to such individual insurrection against pronounced public opinion, compared the Alton mob to the Boston "tea-party," and declared that Lovejoy, "presumptuous and imprudent," had "died as the fool dieth." Phillips, an almost unknown man, took the stand,

and answered in the speech which opens this volume. A more powerful reinforcement could hardly have been looked for; the cause which could find such a defender was henceforth to be feared rather than despised. To the day of his death he was, fully as much as Garrison, the incarnation of the anti-slavery spirit. For this reason his address on the Philosophy of the Abolition Movement, in 1853, has been assigned a place as representing fully the abolition side of the question, just before it was overshadowed by the rise of the Republican party, which opposed only the extension of slavery to the territories.

The history of the sudden development of the anti-slavery struggle in 1845 and the following years, is largely given in the speeches which have been selected to illustrate it. The admission of Texas to the Union in 1845, and the war with Mexico which followed it, resulted in the acquisition of a vast amount of new territory by the United States. From the first suggestion of such an acquisition, the Wilmot proviso (so-called from David Wilmot, of Pennsylvania, who introduced it in Congress), that slavery should be prohibited in the new territory, was persistently offered as an amendment to every bill appropriating money for the purchase of territory from Mexico. It was passed by the House of Representatives, but was balked in the Senate; and the purchase was finally made without any proviso. When the territory came to be organized, the old question came up again: the Wilmot proviso was offered as an amendment. As the territory was now in the possession of the United States, and as it had been acquired in a war whose support had been much more cordial at the South than at the North, the attempt to add the Wilmot proviso to the territorial organization raised the Southern opposition to an intensity which it had not known before. Fuel was added to the flame by the application of California, whose population had been enormously increased by the discovery of gold within her limits, for admission as a free State. If New Mexico should do the same, as was probable, the Wilmot proviso would be practically in force throughout the best portion of the Mexican acquisition. The two sections were now so strong and so determined that compromise of any kind was far more difficult than in 1820; and it was not easy to reconcile or compromise the southern demand that slavery should be permitted, and the northern demand that slavery should be forbidden, to enter the new territories.

In the meantime, the Presidential election of 1848 had come and gone. It had been marked by the appearance of a new party, the Free Soilers, an event which was at first extremely embarrassing to the managers of both the Democratic and Whig parties. On the one hand, the northern and southern sections of the Whig party had always been very loosely joined together, and the slender tie was endangered by the least admission of the slavery issue. On the other hand, while the Democratic national organization had always been more perfect, its northern section had always been much more inclined to active anti-slavery work than the northern Whigs. Its organ, the *Democratic Review*, habitually spoke of the slaves as "our black brethren"; and a long catalogue could be made of leaders like Chase, Hale, Wilmot, Bryant, and Leggett, whose democracy was broad enough to include the negro. To both parties, therefore, the situation was extremely hazardous. The Whigs had less to fear, but were able to resist less pressure. The Democrats were more united, but were called upon to meet a greater danger. In the end, the Whigs did nothing; their two sections drew further apart; and the Presidential election of 1852 only made it evident that the national Whig party was no longer in existence. The Democratic managers evolved, as a solution of their problem, the new doctrine of "popular sovereignty," which Calhoun rebaptized "squatter sovereignty." They asserted as the true Democratic doctrine, that the question of slavery or freedom was to be left for decision of the people of the territory itself. To the mass of northern Democrats, this doctrine was taking enough to cover over the essential nature of the struggle; the more democratic leaders of the northern Democracy were driven off into the Free-Soil party; and Douglas, the champion of "popular sovereignty," became the leading Democrat of the North.

Clay had re-entered the Senate in 1849, for the purpose of compromising the sectional difficulties as he had compromised those of 1820 and of 1833. His speech, as given, will show something of his motives; his success resulted in the "compromise of 1850." By its terms, California was admitted as a free State; the slave trade, but not slavery, was prohibited in the District of Columbia; a more stringent fugitive slave law was enacted; Texas was paid $10,000,000 for certain claims to the Territory of New Mexico; and the Territories of Utah and New Mexico, covering the Mexican acquisition outside of California, were organized without mentioning slavery. The last-named feature was carefully designed to please all important factions. It could be represented to the Webster Whigs that slavery was excluded from the Territories named by the operation of natural laws; to the Clay Whigs that slavery had already been excluded by Mexican law which survived the cession; to the northern Democrats, that the compromise was a formal endorsement of the great principle of popular sovereignty; and to the southern Democrats that it was a repudiation of the Wilmot proviso. In the end, the essence of the success went to the last-named party, for the legislatures of the two territories established slavery, and no bill to veto their action could pass both Houses of Congress until after 1861.

The Supreme Court had already decided that Congress had exclusive power to enforce the fugitive slave clause of the Constitution, though the fugitive slave law of 1793 had given a concurrent authority of execution to State officers. The law of 1850, carrying the Supreme Court's decision further, gave the execution of the law to United States officers, and refused the accused a hearing. Its execution at the North was therefore the occasion of a profound excitement and horror. Cases of inhuman cruelty, and of false accusation to which no defence was permitted, were multiplied until a practical nullification of the law, in the form of "personal liberty laws," securing a hearing for the accused before State magistrates, was forced by public opinion upon the legislature of the exposed northern States. Before the excitement had come to a head, the Whig convention of 1852 met and endorsed the compromise of 1850 "in all its parts." Overwhelmed in the election which followed, the Whig party was popularly said to have "died of an attempt to swallow the fugitive-slave law"; it would have been more correct to have said that the southern section of the party had deserted in a body and gone over to the Democratic party. National politics were thus left in an entirely anomalous condition. The Democratic party was omnipotent at the South, though it was afterward opposed feebly by the American (or "Know Nothing") organization, and was generally successful at the North, though it was still met by the Northern Whigs with vigorous opposition. Such a state of affairs was not calculated to satisfy thinking men; and this period seems to have been one in which very few thinking men of any party were at all satisfied with their party positions.

This was the hazardous situation into which the Democratic managers chose to thrust one of the most momentous pieces of legislation in our political history—the Kansas-Nebraska bill. The responsibility for it is clearly on the shoulders of Stephen A. Douglas. The overland travel to the Pacific coast had made it necessary to remove the Indian title to Kansas and Nebraska, and to organize them as Territories, in order to afford protection to emigrants; and Douglas, chairman of the Senate committee on Territories, introduced a bill for such organization in January, 1854. Both these prospective Territories had been made free soil forever by the compromise of 1820; the question of slavery had been settled, so far as they were concerned; but Douglas consented, after a show of opposition, to reopen Pandora's box. His original bill did not abrogate the Missouri compromise, and there seems to have been no general Southern demand that it should do so. But Douglas had become intoxicated by the unexpected success of his "popular sovereignty" make-shift in regard to the Territories of 1850; and a notice of an amendment to be offered by a southern senator, abrogating the Missouri compromise, was threat or excuse sufficient to bring him to withdraw the bill. A week later, it was reintroduced with the addition of "popular sovereignty": all questions pertaining to slavery in these Territories, and in the States to be formed from them, were to be left to the decision of the people, through their representatives; and the Missouri compromise of 1820 was declared "inoperative and void," as inconsistent with the principles of the territorial legislation of 1850. It must be remembered that the "non-intervention" of 1850 had been confessedly based on no constitutional principle whatever, but was purely a matter of expediency; and that "non-intervention" in Utah and New Mexico was no more inconsistent with the prohibition of slavery in Kansas and Nebraska than "non-intervention" in the Southwest Territory, sixty years before, had been inconsistent with the prohibition of slavery in the Northwest Territory. Whether Douglas is to be considered as too scrupulous, or too timid, or too willing to be terrified, it is certain that his action was unnecessary.

After a struggle of some months, the Kansas-Nebraska bill became law. The Missouri compromise was abrogated, and the question of the extension of slavery to the territories was adrift again, never to be got rid of except through the abolition of slavery itself by war. The demands of the South had now come fully abreast with the proposal of Douglas: that slavery should have *permission* to enter all the Territories, if it could. The opponents of the extension of slavery, at first under the name of "Anti-Nebraska men," then of the Republican party, carried the elections for representatives in Congress in 1854-'55, and narrowly missed carrying the Presidential election of 1856. The percentage of Democratic losses in the congressional districts of the North was sufficient to leave Douglas with hardly any supporters in Congress from his own section. The Democratic party was converted at once into a solid South, with a northern attachment of popular votes which was not sufficient to control very many Congressmen or electoral votes.

Immigration into Kansas was organized at once by leading men of the two sections, with the common design of securing a majority of the voters of the territory and applying "popular sovereignty" for or against slavery. The first sudden inroad of Missouri intruders was successful in securing a pro-slavery legislature and laws; but within two years the stream of free-State immigration had become so powerful, in spite of murder, outrage, and open civil war, that it was very evident that Kansas was to be a free-State. Its expiring territorial legislature endeavored to outwit its constituents by applying for admission as a slave State, under the Lecompton constitution; but the Douglas Democrats could not support the attempt, and it was defeated. Kansas, however, remained a territory until 1861.

The cruelties of this Kansas episode could not but be reflected in the feelings of the two sections and in Congress. In the former it showed too plainly that the divergence of the two sections, indicated in Calhoun's speech of 1850, had widened to an absolute separation in thought, feeling, and purpose. In the latter the debates assumed a virulence which is illustrated by the speeches on the Sumner assault. The current of events had at least carried the sections far enough apart to give striking distance; and the excuse for action was supplied by the Dred Scott decision in 1857.

Dred Scott, a Missouri slave, claiming to be

a free man under the Missouri compromise of 1820, had sued his master, and the case had reached the Supreme Court. A majority of the justices agreed in dismissing the suit; but, as nearly every justice filed an opinion, and as nearly every opinion disagreed with the other opinions on one or more points, it is not easy to see what else is covered by the decision. Nevertheless, the opinion of the Chief Justice, Roger B. Taney, attracted general attention by the strength of its argument and the character of its views. It asserted, in brief, that no slave could become a citizen of the United States, even by enfranchisement or State law; that the prohibition of slavery by the Missouri compromise of 1820 was unconstitutional and void; that the Constitution recognized property in slaves, and was framed for the protection of property; that Congress had no rights or duties in the territories but such as were granted or imposed by the Constitution; and that, therefore, Congress was bound not merely not to forbid slavery, but to actively protect slavery in the Territories. This was just the ground which had always been held by Calhoun, though the South had not supported him in it. Now the South, rejecting Douglas and his " popular sovereignty," was united in its devotion to the decision of the Supreme Court, and called upon the North to yield unhesitating obedience to that body which Webster in 1830 had styled the ultimate arbiter of constitutional questions. This, it was evident, could never be. No respectable authority at the North pretended to uphold the keystone of Taney's argument, that slaves were regarded as property by the Constitution. On the contrary, it was agreed everywhere by those whose opinions were looked to with respect, that slaves were regarded by the Constitution as "persons held to service or labor" under the laws of the State alone; and that the laws of the State could not give such persons a fictitious legal character outside of the State's jurisdiction. Even the Douglas Democrats, who expressed a willingness to yield to the Supreme Court's decision, did not profess to uphold Taney's share in it.

As the Presidential election of 1860 drew near, the evidences of separation became more manifest. The absorption of northern Democrats into the Republican party increased until Douglas, in 1858, narrowly escaped defeat in his contest with Lincoln for a re-election to the Senate from Illinois. In 1860 the Republicans nominated Lincoln for the Presidency on a platform demanding prohibition of slavery in the Territories. The southern delegates seceded from the Democratic convention, and nominated Breckenridge, on a platform demanding congressional protection of slavery in the Territories. The remainder of the Democratic convention nominated Douglas, with a declaration of its willingness to submit to the decision of the Supreme Court on questions of constitutional law. The remnants of the former Whig and American parties, under the name of the Constitutional Union party, nominated Bell without any declaration of principles. Lincoln received a majority of the electoral votes, and became President. His popular vote was a plurality.

Seward's address on the "Irrepressible Conflict," which closes this volume, is representative of the division between the two sections, as it stood just before the actual shock of conflict. Labor systems are delicate things; and that which the South had adopted, of enslaving the laboring class, was one whose influence could not help being universal and aggressive. Every form of energy and prosperity which tended to advance a citizen into the class of representative rulers tended also to make him a slave owner, and to shackle his official policy and purposes with considerations inseparable from his heavy personal interests. Men might divide on other questions at the South; but on this question of slavery the action of the individual had to follow the decisions of a majority which, by the influence of ambitious aspirants for the lead, was continually becoming more aggressive. In constitutional countries, defections to the minority are a steady check upon an aggressive majority; but the southern majority was a steam engine without a safety valve.

In this sense Seward and Lincoln, in 1858, were correct; the labor system of the South was not only a menace to the whole country, but one which could neither decrease nor stand still. It was intolerable by the laws of its being; and it could be got rid of only by allowing a peaceable secession, or by abolishing it through war. The material prosperity which has followed the adoption of the latter alternative, apart from the moral aspects of the case, is enough to show that the South has gained more than all that slavery lost.

WENDELL PHILLIPS,

OF MASSACHUSETTS.

(BORN 1811, DIED 1884.)

ON THE MURDER OF LOVEJOY; FANEUIL HALL, BOSTON, DECEMBER 8, 1837.

MR. CHAIRMAN:

We have met for the freest discussion of these resolutions, and the events which gave rise to them. [Cries of "Question," "Hear him," "Go on," "No gagging," etc.] I hope I shall be permitted to express my surprise at the sentiments of the last speaker, surprise not only at such sentiments from such a man, but at the applause they have received within these walls. A comparison has been drawn between the events of the Revolution and the tragedy at Alton. We have heard it asserted here, in Faneuil Hall, that Great Britain had a right to tax the colonies, and we have heard the mob at Alton, the drunken murderers of Lovejoy, compared to those patriot fathers who threw the tea overboard! Fellow citizens, is this Faneuil Hall doctrine? ["No, no."] The mob at Alton were met to wrest from a citizen his just rights—met to resist the laws. We have been told that our fathers did the same; and the glorious mantle of Revolutionary precedent has been thrown over the mobs of our day. To make out their title to such defence, the gentleman says that the British Parliament had a *right* to tax these colonies. It is manifest that, without this, his parallel falls to the ground, for Lovejoy had stationed himself within constitutional bulwarks. He was not only defending the freedom of the press, but he was under his own roof, in arms with the sanction of the civil authority. The men who assailed him went against and over the laws. The *mob*, as the gentleman terms it—mob, forsooth! certainly we sons of the tea-spillers are a marvellously patient generation!—the "orderly mob" which assembled in the Old South to destroy the tea, were met to resist, not the laws, but illegal enactions. Shame on the American who calls the tea tax and stamp act *laws!* Our fathers resisted, not the King's prerogative, but the King's usurpation. To find any other account, you must read our Revolutionary history up-

side down. Our State archives are loaded
with arguments of John Adams to prove the
taxes laid by the British Parliament unconstitutional—beyond its power. It was not until
this was made out that the men of New England rushed to arms. The arguments of the
Council Chamber and the House of Representatives preceded and sanctioned the contest.
To draw the conduct of our ancestors into a
precedent for mobs, for a right to resist laws we
ourselves have enacted, is an insult to their
memory. The difference between the excitements of those days and our own, which the
gentleman in kindness to the latter has overlooked, is simply this: the men of that day
went for the right, as secured by the laws.
They were the people rising to sustain the laws
and constitution of the Province. The rioters
of our days go for their own wills, right or
wrong. Sir, when I heard the gentleman lay
down principles which place the murderers of
Alton side by side with Otis and Hancock,
with Quincy and Adams, I thought those pictured lips [pointing to the portraits in the
Hall] would have broken into voice to rebuke
the recreant American—the slanderer of the
dead. The gentleman said that he should sink

into insignificance if he dared to gainsay the principles of these resolutions. Sir, for the sentiments he has uttered, on soil consecrated by the prayers of Puritans and the blood of patriots, the earth should have yawned and swallowed him up.

[By this time, the uproar in the Hall had risen so high that the speech was suspended for a short time. Applause and counter applause, cries of " Take that back," " Make him take back recreant," " He sha'n't go on till he takes it back," and counter cries of " Phillips or nobody," continued until the pleadings of well-known citizens had somewhat restored order, when Mr. Phillips resumed.]

Fellow citizens, I cannot take back my words. Surely the Attorney-General, so long and so well known here, needs not the aid of your hisses against one so young as I am—my voice never before heard within these walls! * * *

I must find some fault with the statement which has been made of the events at Alton. It has been asked why Lovejoy and his friends did not appeal to the executive—trust their defence to the police of the city? It has been hinted that, from hasty and ill-judged excitement, the men within the building provoked a quarrel, and that he fell in the course of it, one mob resisting another. Recollect, sir, that they did act with the approbation and sanction of the Mayor. In strict truth, there was no executive to appeal to for protection. The Mayor acknowledged that he could not protect them. They asked him if it was lawful for them to defend themselves. He told them it was, and sanctioned their assembling in arms to do so. They were not, then, a mob; they were not merely citizens defending their own property; they were in some sense the *posse comitatus*, adopted for the occasion into the police of the city, acting under the order of a magistrate. It was civil authority resisting lawless violence. Where, then, was the imprudence? Is the doctrine to be sustained here that it is *imprudent* for men to aid magistrates in executing the laws?

Men are continually asking each other, Had Lovejoy a right to resist? Sir, I protest against the question instead of answering it. Lovejoy did not resist, in the sense they mean. He did not throw himself back on the natural right of self-defence. He did not cry anarchy, and let slip the dogs of civil war, careless of the horrors which would follow. Sir, as I understand this affair, it was not an individual protecting his property; it was not one body of armed men resisting another, and making the streets of a peaceful city run blood with their contentions. It did not bring back the scenes in some old Italian cities, where family met family, and faction met faction, and mutually trampled the laws under foot. No! the men in that house were regularly enrolled, under the sanction of the Mayor. There being no militia in Alton, about seventy men were enrolled with the approbation of the Mayor. These relieved each other every other night. About thirty men were in arms on the night of the sixth, when the press was landed. The next evening, it was not thought necessary to summon more than half that number; among these was Lovejoy. It was, therefore, you perceive, sir, the police of the city resisting rioters—civil government breasting itself to the shock of lawless men.

Here is no question about the right of self-defence. It is in fact simply this: Has the civil magistrate a right to put down a riot?

Some persons seem to imagine that anarchy existed at Alton from the commencement of these disputes. Not at all. "No one of us," says an eyewitness and a comrade of Lovejoy, "has taken up arms during these disturbances but at the command of the Mayor." Anarchy did not settle down on that devoted city till Lovejoy breathed his last. Till then the law, represented in his person, sustained itself against its foes. When he fell, civil authority was trampled under foot. He had "planted himself on his constitutional rights,"—appealed to the laws,—claimed the protection of the civil authority,—taken refuge under "the broad shield of the Constitution. When through that he was pierced and fell, he fell but one sufferer in a common catastrophe." He took refuge under the banner of liberty—amid its folds; and when he fell, its glorious stars and stripes, the emblem of free institutions, around which cluster so many heart-stirring memories, were blotted out in the martyr's blood.

It has been stated, perhaps inadvertently, that Lovejoy or his comrades fired first. This is denied by those who have the best means of knowing. Guns were first fired by the mob. After being twice fired on, those within the building consulted together and deliberately returned the fire. But suppose they did fire first. They had a right so to do; not only the right which every citizen has to defend himself, but the further right which every civil officer has to resist violence. Even if Lovejoy fired the first gun, it would not lessen his claim to our sympathy, or destroy his title to be considered a martyr in defence of a free press. The question now is, Did he act within the constitution and the laws? The men who fell in State Street, on the 5th of March, 1770, did more than Lovejoy is charged with. They were the *first* assailants upon some slight quarrel, they pelted the troops with every missile within reach. Did this bate one jot of the eulogy with which Hancock and Warren hallowed their memory, hailing them as the first martyrs in the cause of American liberty? If, sir, I had adopted what are called Peace principles, I might lament the circumstances of this case. But all you who believe as I do, in the right and duty of magistrates to execute the laws, join with me and brand as base hypocrisy the conduct of those who assemble year after year on the 4th of July to fight over the battles of the Revolution, and yet "damn with faint praise" or load with obloquy, the memory of this man who shed his blood in defence of life, liberty, property, and the freedom of the press!

Throughout that terrible night I find nothing to regret but this, that, within the limits of our country, civil authority should have been so prostrated as to oblige a citizen to arm in his own defence, and to arm in vain. The gentleman says Lovejoy was presumptuous and imprudent —he "died as the fool dieth." And a reverend clergyman of the city tells us that no citizen has a right to publish opinions disagreeable to the community! If any mob follows such publication, on *him* rests its guilt. He must wait, forsooth, till the people come up to it and agree with him! This libel on liberty goes on to say that the want of right to speak as we think is an evil inseparable from republican institutions! If this be so, what are they worth? Welcome the despotism of the Sultan, where one knows what he may publish and what he may not, rather than the tyranny of this many-headed monster, the mob, where we know not what we may do or say, till some fellow-citizen has tried it, and paid for the lesson with his life. This clerical absurdity chooses as a check for the abuses of the press, not the *law*, but the dread of a mob. By so doing, it deprives not only the individual and the minority of their rights, but the majority also, since the expression of *their* opinion may sometime provoke disturbances from the minority. A few men may make a mob as well as many. The majority then, have no right, as Christian men, to utter their sentiments, if by any possibility it may lead to a mob! Shades of Hugh Peters and John Cotton, save us from such pulpits!

Imprudent to defend the liberty of the press! Why? Because the defence was unsuccessful? Does success gild crime into patriotism, and the want of it change heroic self-devotion to imprudence? Was Hampden imprudent when he drew the sword and threw away the scabbard? Yet he, judged by that single hour, was unsuccessful. After a short exile, the race he hated sat again upon the throne.

Imagine yourself present when the first news of Bunker Hill battle reached a New England town. The tale would have run thus: "The patriots are routed,—the redcoats victorious,—Warren lies dead upon the field." With what scorn would that *Tory* have been received, who should have charged Warren with *imprudence!* who should have said that, bred a physician, he was "out of place" in that battle, and "died as the *fool dieth*." How would the intimation have been received, that Warren and his associates should have merited a better time? But if success be indeed the only criterion of prudence, *Respice finem*,—wait till the end!

Presumptuous to assert the freedom of the press on American ground! Is the assertion of such freedom before the age? So much before the age as to leave one no right to make it because it displeases the community? Who invents this libel on his country? It is this very thing which entitles Lovejoy to greater praise. The disputed right which provoked the Revolution—taxation without representation—is far beneath that for which he died. [Here there was a general expression of strong disapprobation.] One word, gentlemen. As much as *thought* is better than money, so much is the cause in which Lovejoy died nobler than a mere question of taxes. James Otis thundered in this hall when the King did but touch his *pocket*. Imagine, if you can, his indignant eloquence had England offered to put a gag upon his *lips*. The question that stirred the Revolution touched our civil interests. This concerns us not only as citizens, but as immortal beings. Wrapped up in its fate, saved or lost with it, are not only the voice of the statesman, but the instructions of the pulpit and the progress of our faith.

The clergy, "marvellously out of place" where free speech is battled for—liberty of speech on national sins! Does the gentleman remember that freedom to preach was first gained, dragging in its train freedom to print? I thank the clergy here present, as I reverence their predecessors, who did not so far forget their country in their immediate profession as to deem it duty to separate themselves from the struggle of '76—the Mayhews and Coopers, who remembered that they were citizens before they were clergymen.

Mr. Chairman, from the bottom of my heart I thank that brave little band at Alton for resisting. We must remember that Lovejoy had fled from city to city,—suffered the destruction of three presses patiently. At length he took counsel with friends, men of character, of tried integrity, of wide views, of Christian principle. They thought the crisis had come; it was full time to assert the laws. They saw around them, not a community like our own, of fixed habits, of character moulded and settled, but one "in the gristle, not yet hardened into the bone of manhood." The people there, children of our older States, seem to have forgotten the blood-tried principles of their fathers the moment they lost sight of our New England hills. Something was to be done to show them the priceless value of the freedom of the press, to bring back and set right their wandering and confused ideas. He and his advisers looked out on a community, staggering like a drunken man, indifferent to their rights and confused in their feelings. Deaf to argument, haply they might be stunned into sobriety. They saw that of which we cannot judge, the *necessity* of resistance. Insulted law called for it. Public opinion, fast hastening on the downward course, must be arrested.

Does not the event show they judged rightly? Absorbed in a thousand trifles, how has the nation all at once come to a stand? Men begin, as in 1776 and 1640, to discuss principles, to weigh characters, to find out where they are. Haply we may awake before we are borne over the precipice.

I am glad, sir, to see this crowded house, It is good for us to be here. When Liberty is in danger Faneuil Hall has the right, it is her duty, to strike the key-note for these United States. I am glad, for one reason, that remarks such as those to which I have alluded have been uttered here. The passage of these resolutions, in spite of this opposition, led by the Attorney-General of the Commonwealth, will show more clearly, more decisively, the deep indignation with which Boston regards this outrage.

JOHN C. CALHOUN,

OF SOUTH CAROLINA.

(BORN 1782, DIED 1850.)

ON THE SLAVERY QUESTION, SENATE, MARCH 4, 1850.

I HAVE, Senators, believed from the first that the agitation of the subject of slavery would, if not prevented by some timely and effective measure, end in disunion. Entertaining this opinion, I have, on all proper occasions, endeavored to call the attention of both the two great parties which divide the country to adopt some measure to prevent so great a disaster, but without success. The agitation has been permitted to proceed, with almost no attempt to resist it, until it has reached a point when it can no longer be disguised or denied that the Union is in danger. You have thus had forced upon you the greatest and the gravest question that can ever come under your consideration: How can the Union be preserved?

To give a satisfactory answer to this mighty question, it is indispensable to have an accurate and thorough knowledge of the nature and the character of the cause by which the Union is endangered. Without such knowledge it is impossible to pronounce, with any certainty, by what measure it can be saved; just as it would be impossible for a physician to pronounce, in the case of some dangerous disease, with any certainty, by what remedy the patient could be saved, without similar knowledge of the nature and character of the cause which produced it. The first question, then, presented for consideration, in the investigation I propose to make, in order to obtain such knowledge, is: What is it that has endangered the Union?

To this question there can be but one answer: That the immediate cause is the almost universal discontent which pervades all the States composing the southern section of the Union. This widely-extended discontent is not of recent origin. It commenced with the agitation of the slavery question, and has been increasing ever since. The next question, going one step further back, is: What has caused this widely-diffused and almost universal discontent?

It is a great mistake to suppose, as is by some, that it originated with demagogues, who excited the discontent with the intention of aiding their personal advancement, or with the disappointed ambition of certain politicians, who resorted to it as a means of retrieving their fortunes. On the contrary, all the great political influences of the section were arrayed against excitement, and exerted to the utmost to keep the people quiet. The great mass of the people of the South were divided, as in the other section, into Whigs and Democrats. The leaders and the presses of both parties in the South were very solicitous to prevent excitement and to preserve quiet; because it was seen that the effects of the former would necessarily tend to weaken, if not destroy, the political ties which united them with their respective parties in the other section. Those who know the strength of the party ties will readily appreciate the immense force which this cause exerted against agitation, and in favor of preserving quiet. But, great as it was, it was not sufficient to prevent the wide-spread discontent which now pervades the section. No; some cause, far deeper and more powerful than the one supposed, must exist, to account for discontent so wide and deep. The question then recurs: What is the cause of this discontent? It will be found in the belief of the people of the Southern States, as prevalent as the discontent itself, that they cannot remain, as things now are, consistently with honor and safety, in the Union. The next question to be considered is: What has caused this belief?

One of the causes is, undoubtedly, to be traced to the long-continued agitation of the slavery question on the part of the North, and the many aggressions which they have made on the rights of the South during the time. I will not enumerate them at present, as it will be done hereafter in its proper place.

There is another lying back of it—with which this is intimately connected—that may be regarded as the great and primary cause. This is to be found in the fact, that the equilibrium between the two sections, in the Government as it stood when the Constitution was ratified and the Government put in action, has been destroyed. At that time there was nearly a perfect equilibrium between the two, which afforded ample means to each to protect itself against the aggression of the other; but, as it now stands, one section has the exclusive power of controlling the Government, which leaves the other without any adequate means of protecting itself against its encroachment and oppression. To place this subject distinctly before you, I have, Senators, prepared a brief statistical statement, showing the relative weight of the two sections in the Government under the first census of 1790, and the last census of 1840.

According to the former, the population of the United States, including Vermont, Kentucky, and Tennessee, which then were in their incipient condition of becoming States, but were not actually admitted, amounted to 3,929,827. Of this number the Northern States had 1,997,899, and the Southern 1,952,072, making a difference of only 45,827 in favor of the former States.

The number of States, including Vermont, Kentucky, and Tennessee, were sixteen; of which eight, including Vermont, belonged to the northern section, and eight, including Kentucky and Tennessee, to the southern,—making an equal division of the States between the two sections, under the first census. There was a small preponderance in the House of Representatives, and in the Electoral College, in favor of the northern, owing to the fact that, according to the provisions of the Constitution, in estimating federal numbers five slaves count but three; but it was too small to affect sensibly the perfect equilibrium which, with that exception, existed at the time. Such was the equality of the two sections when the States composing them agreed to enter into a Federal Union. Since then the equilibrium between them has been greatly disturbed.

According to the last census the aggregate population of the United States amounted to 17,063,357, of which the northern section contained 9,728,920, and the southern 7,334,437, making a difference in round numbers, of 2,400,000. The number of States had increased from sixteen to twenty-six, making an addition of ten States. In the meantime the position of Delaware had become doubtful as to which section she properly belonged. Considering her as neutral, the Northern States will have thirteen and the Southern States twelve, making a difference in the Senate of two senators in favor of the former. According to the apportionment under the census of 1840, there were two hundred and twenty-three members of the House of Representatives, of which the Northern States had one hundred and thirty-five, and the Southern States (considering Delaware as neutral) eighty-seven, making a difference in favor of the former in the House of Representatives of forty-eight. The difference in the Senate of two members, added to this, gives to the North in the Electoral College, a majority of fifty. Since the census of 1840, four States have been added to the Union—Iowa, Wisconsin, Florida, and Texas. They leave the difference in the Senate as it was when the census was taken; but add two to the side of the North in the House, making the present majority in the House in its favor fifty, and in the Electoral College fifty-two.

The result of the whole is to give the northern section a predominance in every department of the Government, and thereby concentrate in it the two elements which constitute the Federal Government,—majority of States, and a majority of their population, estimated in federal numbers. Whatever section concentrates the two in itself possesses the control of the entire Government.

But we are just at the close of the sixth decade, and the commencement of the seventh. The census is to be taken this year, which must add greatly to the decided preponderance of the North in the House of Representatives and in the Electoral College. The prospect is, also, that a great increase will be added to its present preponderance in the Senate, during the period of the decade, by the addition of new States. Two territories, Oregon and Minnesota, are already in progress, and strenuous efforts are making to bring in three additional States from the territory recently conquered from Mexico; which, if successful, will add three other States in a short time to the northern section, making five States; and increasing the present number of its States from fifteen to twenty, and of its senators from thirty to forty. On the contrary, there is not a single territory in progress in the southern section, and no certainty that any additional State will be added to it during the decade. The prospect then is, that the two sections in the senate, should the effort now made to exclude the South from the newly acquired territories succeed, will stand before the end of the decade, twenty Northern States to fourteen Southern (considering Delaware as neutral), and forty Northern senators to twenty-eight Southern. This great increase of senators, added to the great increase of members of the House of Representatives and the Electoral

College on the part of the North, which must take place under the next decade, will effectually and irretrievably destroy the equilibrium which existed when the Government commenced.

Had this destruction been the operation of time, without the interference of Government, the South would have had no reason to complain; but such was not the fact. It was caused by the legislation of this Government, which was appointed as the common agent of all, and charged with the protection of the interests and security of all. The legislation by which it has been effected may be classed under three heads. The first is, that series of acts by which the South has been excluded from the common territory belonging to all the States as members of the Federal Union—which have had the effect of extending vastly the portion allotted to the northern section, and restricting within narrow limits the portion left the South. The next consists in adopting a system of revenue and disbursements, by which an undue proportion of the burden of taxation has been imposed upon the South, and an undue proportion of its proceeds appropriated to the North; and the last is a system of political measures, by which the original character of the Government has been radically changed. I propose to bestow upon each of these, in the order they stand, a few remarks, with the view of showing that it is owing to the action of this Government that the equilibrium between the two sections has been destroyed, and the whole powers of the system centered in a sectional majority.

The first of the series of Acts by which the South was deprived of its due share of the territories, originated with the confederacy which preceded the existence of this Government. It is to be found in the provision of the ordinance of 1787. Its effect was to exclude the South entirely from that vast and fertile region which lies between the Ohio and the Mississippi rivers, now embracing five States and one Territory. The next of the series is the Missouri compromise, which excluded the South from that large portion of Louisiana which lies north of 36° 30', excepting what is included in the State of Missouri. The last of the series excluded the South from the whole of Oregon Territory. All these, in the slang of the day, were what are called slave territories, and not free soil; that is, territories belonging to slaveholding powers and open to the emigration of masters with their slaves. By these several Acts the South was excluded from one million two hundred and thirty-eight thousand and twenty-five square miles—an extent of country considerably exceeding the entire valley of the Mississippi. To the South was left the portion of the Territory of Louisiana lying south of 36° 30', and the portion north of it included in the State of Missouri, with the portion lying south of 36° 30' including the States of Louisiana and Arkansas, and the territory lying west of the latter, and south of 36° 30', called the Indian country. These, with the Territory of Florida, now the State, make, in the whole, two hundred and eighty-three thousand five hundred and three square miles. To this must be added the territory acquired with Texas. If the whole should be added to the southern section it would make an increase of three hundred and twenty-five thousand five hundred and twenty, which would make the whole left to the South six hundred and nine thousand and twenty-three. But a large part of Texas is still in contest between the two sections, which leaves it uncertain what will be the real extent of the proportion of territory that may be left to the South.

I have not included the territory recently acquired by the treaty with Mexico. The North is making the most strenuous efforts to appropriate the whole to herself, by excluding the South from every foot of it. If she should succeed, it will add to that from which the South has already been excluded, 526,078 square miles, and would increase the whole which the North has appropriated to herself, to 1, 764,023, not including the portion that she may succeed in excluding us from in Texas. To sum up the whole, the United States, since they declared their independence, have acquired 2,373,046 square miles of territory, from which the North will have excluded the South, if she should succeed in monopolizing the newly acquired territories, about three fourths of the whole, leaving to the South but about one fourth.

Such is the first and great cause that has destroyed the equilibrium between the two sections in the Government.

The next is the system of revenue and disbursements which has been adopted by the Government. It is well known that the Government has derived its revenue mainly from duties on imports. I shall not undertake to show that such duties must necessarily fall mainly on the exporting States, and that the South, as the great exporting portion of the Union, has in reality paid vastly more than her due proportion of the revenue; because I deem it unnecessary, as the subject has on so many occasions been fully discussed. Nor shall I, for the same reason, undertake to show that a far greater portion of the revenue has been disbursed at the North, than its due share; and that the joint effect of these causes has been, to transfer a vast amount from South to North, which, under an equal system of revenue and disbursements, would not have been lost to her. If to this be added, that many of the duties were imposed, not for revenue, but for protection,—that is, intended to put money, not in the treasury, but directly into the pockets of the manufacturers,—some conception may be formed of the immense amount which, in the long course of sixty years, has been transferred from South to North. There are no data by which it can be estimated with any certainty; but it is safe to say that it amounts to hundreds of millions of dollars. Under the most moderate estimate, it would be sufficient to add greatly to the wealth of the North, and thus greatly increase her population by attracting emigration from all quarters to that section.

This, combined with the great primary cause, amply explains why the North has acquired a preponderance in every department of the Government by its disproportionate increase of population and States. The former, as has been shown, has increased, in fifty years, 2,400,000 over that of the South. This increase of population, during so long a period, is satisfactorily accounted for, by the number of emigrants, and the increase of their descendants, which have been attracted to the northern section from Europe and the South, in consequence of the advantages derived from the causes assigned. If they had not existed—if the South had retained all the capital which had been extracted from her by the fiscal action of the Government; and, if it had not been excluded by the ordinance of 1787 and the Missouri compromise, from the region lying between the Ohio and the Mississippi rivers, and between the Mississippi and the Rocky Mountains north of 36° 30′—it scarcely admits of a doubt, that it would have divided the emigration with the North, and by retaining her own people, would have at least equalled the North in population under the census of 1840, and probably under that about to be taken. She would also, if she had retained her equal rights in those territories, have maintained an equality in the number of States with the North, and have preserved the equilibrium between the two sections that existed at the commencement of the Government. The loss, then, of the equilibrium is to be attributed to the action of this Government.

But while these measures were destroying the equilibrium between the two sections, the action of the Government was leading to a radical change in its character, by concentrating all the power of the system in itself. The occasion will not permit me to trace the measures by which this great change has been consummated. If it did, it would not be difficult to show that the process commenced at an early period of the Government; and that it proceeded, almost without interruption, step by step, until it virtually absorbed its entire powers; but without going through the whole process to establish the fact, it may be done satisfactorily by a very short statement.

That the Government claims, and practically maintains, the right to decide in the last resort, as to the extent of its powers, will scarcely be denied by any one conversant with the political history of the country. That it also claims the right to resort to force to maintain whatever power it claims against all opposition is equally certain. Indeed it is apparent, from what we daily hear, that this has become the prevailing and fixed opinion of a great majority of the community. Now, I ask, what limitation can possibly be placed upon the powers of a government claiming and exercising such rights? And, if none can be, how can the separate governments of the States maintain and protect the powers reserved to them by the Constitution— or the people of the several States maintain those which are reserved to them, and among others, the sovereign powers by which they ordained and established, not only their separate State Constitutions and Governments, but also the Constitution and Government of the United States? But, if they have no constitutional means of maintaining them against the right claimed by this Government, it necessarily follows, that they hold them at its pleasure and discretion, and that all the powers of the system are in reality concentrated in it. It also follows, that the character of the Government has been changed in consequence, from a federal republic, as it originally came from the hands of its framers, into a great national consolidated democracy. It has indeed, at present, all the characteristics of the latter, and not of the former, although it still retains its outward form.

The result of the whole of those causes combined is, that the North has acquired a decided ascendency over every department of this Government, and through it a control over all the powers of the system. A single section governed by the will of the numerical majority, has now, in fact, the control of the Government and the entire powers of the system. What was once a constitutional federal republic, is now converted, in reality, into one as absolute as that of the Autocrat of Russia, and as despotic in its tendency as any absolute government that ever existed.

As, then, the North has the absolute control over the Government, it is manifest that on all questions between it and the South, where there is a diversity of interests, the interest of the latter will be sacrificed to the former, however oppressive the effects may be; as the South possesses no means by which it can resist, through the action of the Government. But if there was no question of vital importance to the South, in reference to which there was a diversity of views between the two sections, this state of things might be endured without the hazard of destruction to the South. But such is not the fact. There is a question of vital importance to the southern section, in reference to which the views and feelings of the two sections are as opposite and hostile as they can possibly be.

I refer to the relation between the two races in the southern section, which constitutes a vital portion of her social organization. Every portion of the North entertains views and feelings more or less hostile to it. Those most opposed and hostile, regard it as a sin, and consider themselves under the most sacred obligation to use every effort to destroy it. Indeed, to the extent that they conceive that they have power, they regard themselves as implicated in the sin, and responsible for not suppressing it by the use of all and every means. Those less opposed and hostile, regarded it as a crime—an offence against humanity, as they call it; and, although not so fanatical, feel themselves bound to use all efforts to effect the same object; while those who are least opposed and hostile, regard it as a blot and a stain on the character of what they call the Nation, and feel themselves accordingly bound to give it no countenance or support. On the contrary, the southern section regards the relation as one which cannot be destroyed without subjecting the two races to the greatest calamity, and the section to poverty, desolation, and wretchedness; and accordingly they feel bound, by every consideration of interest and safety, to defend it.

This hostile feeling on the part of the North toward the social organization of the South long lay dormant, and it only required some cause to act on those who felt most intensely that they were responsible for its continuance, to call it into action. The increasing power of this Government, and of the control of the northern section over all its departments, furnished the cause. It was this which made the impression on the minds of many, that there was little or no restraint to prevent the Government from doing whatever it might choose to do. This was sufficient of itself to put the most fanatical portion of the North in action, for the purpose of destroying the existing relation between the two races in the South.

The first organized movement toward it commenced in 1835. Then, for the first time, societies were organized, presses established, lecturers sent forth to excite the people of the North, and incendiary publications scattered over the whole South, through the mail. The South was thoroughly aroused. Meetings were held everywhere, and resolutions adopted, calling upon the North to apply a remedy to arrest the threatened evil, and pledging themselves to adopt measures for their own protection, if it was not arrested. At the meeting of Congress, petitions poured in from the North, calling upon Congress to abolish slavery in the District of Columbia, and to prohibit, what they called, the internal slave trade between the States—announcing at the same time, that their ultimate object was to abolish slavery, not only in the District, but in the States and throughout the Union. At this period, the number engaged in the agitation was small, and possessed little or no personal influence.

Neither party in Congress had, at that time, any sympathy with them or their cause. The members of each party presented their petitions with great reluctance. Nevertheless, small, and contemptible as the party then was, both of the great parties of the North dreaded them. They felt, that though small, they were organized in reference to a subject which had a great and commanding influence over the northern mind. Each party, on that account, feared to oppose their petitions, lest the opposite party should take advantage of the one who might do so, by favoring them. The effect was, that both united in insisting that the petitions should be received, and that Congress should take jurisdiction over the subject. To justify their course, they took the extraordinary ground, that Congress was bound to receive petitions on every subject, however objectionable they might be, and whether they had, or had not, jurisdiction over the subject. Those views prevailed in the House of Representatives, and partially in the Senate; and thus the party succeeded in their first movements, in gaining what they proposed—a position in Congress, from which agitation could be extended over the whole Union. This was the commencement of the agitation, which has ever since continued, and which, as is now acknowledged, has endangered the Union itself.

As for myself, I believed at that early period, if the party who got up the petitions should succeed in getting Congress to take jurisdiction, that agitation would follow, and that it would in the end, if not arrested, destroy the Union. I then so expressed myself in debate, and called upon both parties to take grounds against assuming jurisdiction; but in vain. Had my voice been heeded, and had Congress refused to take jurisdiction, by the united votes of all parties, the agitation which followed would have been prevented, and the fanatical zeal that gave impulse to the agitation, and which has brought us to our present perilous condition, would have become extinguished, from the want of fuel to feed the flame. *That* was the time for the North to have shown her devotion to the Union; but, unfortunately, both of the great parties of that section were so intent on obtaining or retaining party ascendency, that all other considerations were overlooked or forgotten.

What has since followed are but natural consequences. With the success of their first movement, this small fanatical party began to acquire strength; and with that, to become an object of courtship to both the great parties. The necessary consequence was, a further increase of power, and a gradual tainting of the opinions of both the other parties with their doctrines, until the infection has extended over both; and the great mass of the population of the North, who, whatever may be their opinion of the original abolition party, which still preserves its distinctive organization, hardly ever fail, when it comes to acting, to co-operate in carrying out their measures. With the increase of their influence, they extended the sphere of their action. In a short time after the commencement of their first movement, they had acquired sufficient influence to induce the legislatures of most of the Northern States to pass acts, which in effect abrogated the clause of the Constitution that provides for the delivery up of fugitive slaves. Not long after, petitions followed to abolish slavery in forts, magazines, and dockyards, and all other places where Congress had exclusive power of legislation. This was followed by petitions and resolutions of legislatures of the Northern States, and popular meetings, to exclude the Southern States from all territories acquired, or to be acquired, and to prevent the admission of any State hereafter into the Union, which, by its constitution, does not prohibit slavery. And Congress is invoked to do all this, expressly with the view of the final abolition of slavery in the States. That has been avowed to be the ultimate object from the beginning of the agitation until the present time; and yet the great body of both parties of the North, with the full knowledge of the fact, although disavowing the abolitionists, have co-operated with them in almost all their measures.

Such is a brief history of the agitation, as far as it has yet advanced. Now I ask, Senators, what is there to prevent its further progress, until it fulfils the ultimate end proposed, unless some decisive measure should be adopted to prevent it? Has any one of the causes, which has added to its increase from its original small and contemptible beginning until it has attained its present magnitude, diminished in force? Is the original cause of the movement—that slavery is a sin, and ought to be suppressed—weaker now than at the commencement? Or is the abolition party less numerous or influential, or have they less influence with, or less control over the two great parties of the North in elections? Or has the South greater means of influencing or controlling the movements of this Government now, than it had when the agitation commenced? To all these questions but one answer can be given: No, no, no. The very reverse is true. Instead of being weaker, all the elements in favor of agitation are stronger now than they were in 1835, when it first commenced, while all the elements of influence on the part of the South are weaker. Unless something decisive is done, I again ask, what is to stop this agitation, before the great and final object at which it aims—the abolition of slavery in the States—is consummated? Is it, then, not certain, that if something is not done to arrest it, the South will be forced to choose between abolition and secession? Indeed, as events are now moving, it will not require the South to secede, in order to dissolve the Union. Agitation will of itself effect it, of which its past history furnishes abundant proof—as I shall next proceed to show.

It is a great mistake to suppose that disunion can be effected by a single blow. The cords which bound these States together in one common Union, are far too numerous and powerful for that. Disunion must be the work of time. It is only through a long process, and successively, that the cords can be snapped, until the whole fabric falls asunder. Already the agitation of the slavery question has snapped some of the most important, and has greatly weakened all the others, as I shall proceed to show.

The cords that bind the States together are not only many, but various in character. Some are spiritual or ecclesiastical; some political; others social. Some appertain to the benefit conferred by the Union, and others to the feeling of duty and obligation.

The strongest of those of a spiritual and ecclesiastical nature, consisted in the unity of the great religious denominations, all of which originally embraced the whole Union. All these denominations, with the exception, perhaps, of the Catholics, were organized very much upon the principle of our political institutions. Beginning with smaller meetings, corresponding with the political divisions of the country, their organization terminated in one great central assemblage, corresponding very much with the character of Congress. At these meetings the principal clergymen and lay members of the respective denominations from all parts of the Union, met to transact business relating to their common concerns. It was not confined to what appertained to the doctrines and discipline of the respective denominations, but extended to plans for disseminating the Bible—establishing missions, distributing tracts —and of establishing presses for the publication of tracts, newspapers, and periodicals, with a view of diffusing religious information—and for the support of their respective doctrines and creeds. All this combined contributed greatly to strengthen the bonds of the Union. The ties which held each denomination together formed a strong cord to hold the whole Union together, but, powerful as they were, they have not been able to resist the explosive effect of slavery agitation.

The first of these cords which snapped, under its explosive force, was that of the powerful Methodist Episcopal Church. The numerous and strong ties which held it together, are all broken, and its unity is gone. They now form separate churches; and, instead of that feeling of attachment and devotion to the interests of the whole church which was formerly felt, they are now arrayed into two hostile bodies, engaged in litigation about what was formerly their common property.

The next cord that snapped was that of the Baptists—one of the largest and most respectable of the denominations. That of the Presbyterian is not entirely snapped, but some of its strands have given way. That of the Episcopal Church is the only one of the four great

Protestant denominations which remains unbroken and entire.

The strongest cord, of a political character, consists of the many and powerful ties that have held together the two great parties which have, with some modifications, existed from the beginning of the Government. They both extended to every portion of the Union, and strongly contributed to hold all its parts together. But this powerful cord has fared no better than the spiritual. It resisted, for a long time, the explosive tendency of the agitation, but has finally snapped under its force—if not entirely, in a great measure. Nor is there one of the remaining cords which has not been greatly weakened. To this extent the Union has already been destroyed by agitation, in the only way it can be, by sundering and weakening the cords which bind it together.

If the agitation goes on, the same force, acting with increased intensity, as has been shown, will finally snap every cord, when nothing will be left to hold the States together except force. But, surely, that can, with no propriety of language, be called a Union, when the only means by which the weaker is held connected with the stronger portion is *force*. It may, indeed, keep them connected; but the connection will partake much more of the character of subjugation, on the part of the weaker to the stronger, than the union of free, independent States, in one confederation, as they stood in the early stages of the Government, and which only is worthy of the sacred name of Union.

Having now, Senators, explained what it is that endangers the Union, and traced it to its cause, and explained its nature and character, the question again recurs, How can the Union be saved? To this I answer, there is but one way by which it can be, and that is by adopting such measures as will satisfy the States belonging to the southern section, that they can remain in the Union consistently with their honor and their safety. There is, again, only one way by which this can be effected, and that is by removing the causes by which this belief has been produced. Do *this*, and discontent will cease, harmony and kind feelings between the sections be restored, and every apprehension of danger to the Union be removed. The question, then, is, How can this be done? But, before I undertake to answer this question, I propose to show by what the Union cannot be saved.

It cannot, then, be saved by eulogies on the Union, however splendid or numerous. The cry of "Union, Union, the glorious Union!" can no more prevent disunion than the cry of "Health, health, glorious health!" on the part of the physician, can save a patient lying dangerously ill. So long as the Union, instead of being regarded as a protector, is regarded in the opposite character, by not much less than a majority of the States, it will be in vain to attempt to conciliate them by pronouncing eulogies on it.

Besides, this cry of Union comes commonly from those whom we cannot believe to be sincere. It usually comes from our assailants. But we cannot believe them to be sincere; for, if they loved the Union, they would necessarily be devoted to the Constitution. It made the Union,—and to destroy the Constitution would be to destroy the Union. But the only reliable and certain evidence of devotion to the Constitution is to abstain, on the one hand, from violating it, and to repel, on the other, all attempts to violate it. It is only by faithfully performing these high duties that the Constitution can be preserved, and with it the Union.

But how stands the profession of devotion to

the Union by our assailants, when brought to this test? Have they abstained from violating the Constitution? Let the many acts passed by the Northern States to set aside and annul the clause of the Constitution providing for the delivery up of fugitive slaves answer. I cite this, not that it is the only instance (for there are many others), but because the violation in this particular is too notorious and palpable to be denied. Again: Have they stood forth faithfully to repel violations of the Constitution? Let their course in reference to the agitation of the slavery question, which was commenced and has been carried on for fifteen years, avowedly for the purpose of abolishing slavery in the States—an object all acknowledged to be unconstitutional,—answer. Let them show a single instance, during this long period, in which they have denounced the agitators or their attempts to effect what is admitted to be unconstitutional, or a single measure which they have brought forward for that purpose. How can we, with all these facts before us, believe that they are sincere in their profession of devotion to the Union, or avoid believing their profession is but intended to increase the vigor of their assaults and to weaken the force of our resistance?

Nor can we regard the profession of devotion to the Union, on the part of those who are not our assailants, as sincere, when they pronounce eulogies upon the Union, evidently with the intent of charging us with disunion, without uttering one word of denunciation against our assailants. If friends of the Union, their course should be to unite with us in repelling these assaults, and denouncing the authors as enemies of the Union. Why they avoid this, and pursue the course they do, it is for them to explain.

Nor can the Union be saved by invoking the name of the illustrious Southerner whose mortal remains repose on the western bank of the Potomac. He was one of us,—a slaveholder and a planter. We have studied his history, and find nothing in it to justify submission to wrong. On the contrary, his great fame rests on the solid foundation, that, while he was careful to avoid doing wrong to others, he was prompt and decided in repelling wrong. I trust that, in this respect, we profited by his example.

Nor can we find any thing in his history to deter us from seceding from the Union, should it fail to fulfil the objects for which it was instituted, by being permanently and hopelessly converted into the means of oppressing instead of protecting us. On the contrary, we find much in his example to encourage us, should we be forced to the extremity of deciding between submission and disunion.

There existed then, as well as now, a union —between the parent country and her colonies. It was a union that had much to endear it to the people of the colonies. Under its protecting and superintending care, the colonies were planted and grew up and prospered, through a long course of years, until they became populous and wealthy. Its benefits were not limited to them. Their extensive agricultural and other productions, gave birth to a flourishing commerce, which richly rewarded the parent country for the trouble and expense of establishing and protecting them. Washington was born and grew up to manhood under that Union. He acquired his early distinction in its service, and there is every reason to believe that he was devotedly attached to it. But his devotion was a national one. He was attached to it, not as an end, but as a means to an end. When it failed to fulfil its end, and, instead of affording protection, was converted into the means of oppressing the colonies, he did not hesitate to draw his sword, and head the great movement by which that union was forever severed, and the independence of these States established. This was the great and crowning glory of his life, which has spread his fame over the whole globe, and will transmit it to the latest posterity.

Nor can the plan proposed by the distinguished Senator from Kentucky, nor that of the administration, save the Union. I shall pass by, without remark, the plan proposed by the Senator. I, however, assure the distinguished and able Senator, that, in taking this course, no disrespect whatever is intended to him or to his plan. I have adopted it because so many Senators of distinguished abilities, who were present when he delivered his speech, and explained his plan, and who were fully capable to do justice to the side they support, have replied to him. * * *

Having now shown what cannot save the Union, I return to the question with which I commenced, How can the Union be saved? There is but one way by which it can with any certainty; and that is, by a full and final settlement, on the principle of justice, of all the questions at issue between the two sections. The South asks for justice, simple justice, and less she ought not to take. She has no compromise to offer, but the Constitution; and no concession or surrender to make. She has already surrendered so much that she has little left to surrender. Such a settlement would go to the root of the evil, and remove all cause of discontent, by satisfying the South that she could remain honorably and safely in the Union, and thereby restore the harmony and fraternal feelings between the sections, which existed anterior to the Missouri agitation. Nothing else can, with any certainty, finally and forever settle the question at issue, terminate agitation, and save the Union.

But can this be done? Yes, easily; not by the weaker party, for it can, of itself do nothing, —not even protect itself—but by the stronger. The North has only to will it to accomplish it —to do justice by conceding to the South an equal right in the acquired territory, and to do her duty by causing the stipulations relative to fugitive slaves to be faithfully fulfilled, to cease the agitation of the slave question, and to provide for the insertion of a provision in the Constitution, by an amendment, which will restore to the South, in substance, the power she possessed of protecting herself, before the equilibrium between the sections was destroyed by the action of this Government. There will be no difficulty in devising such a provision—one that will protect the South, and which, at the same time, will improve and strengthen the Government, instead of impairing and weakening it.'

But will the North agree to this? It is for her to answer the question. But, I will say, she cannot refuse, if she has half the love for the Union which she professes to have, or without justly exposing herself to the charge that her love of power and aggrandizement is far greater than her love of the Union. At all events the responsibility of saving the Union rests on the North, and not on the South. The South cannot save it by any act of hers, and the North may save it without any sacrifice whatever, unless to do justice, and to perform her duties under the Constitution, should be regarded by her as a sacrifice.

It is time, Senators, that there should be an open and manly avowal on all sides, as to what is intended to be done. If the question is not now settled, it is uncertain whether it ever can hereafter be; and we, as the representatives of the States of this Union, regarded as governments, should come to a distinct understanding as to our respective views, in order to ascertain whether the great questions at issue can be settled or not. If you, who represent the stronger portion, cannot agree to settle on the broad principle of justice and duty, say so; and let the States we both represent agree to separate and part in peace. If you are unwilling we should part in peace, tell us so, and we shall know what to do, when you reduce the question to submission or resistance. If you remain silent, you will compel us to infer by your acts what you intend. In that case, California will become the test question. If you admit her, under all the difficulties that oppose her admission, you compel us to infer that you intend to exclude us from the whole of the acquired territories, with the intention of destroying, irretrievably, the equilibrium between the two sections. We would be blind not to perceive in that case, that your real objects are power and aggrandizement, and infatuated, not to act accordingly.

I have now, Senators, done my duty in expressing my opinions fully, freely and candidly, on this solemn occasion. In doing so, I have been governed by the motives which have governed me in all the stages of the agitation of the slavery question since its commencement. I have exerted myself, during the whole period, to arrest it, with the intention of saving the Union, if it could be done; and if it could not, to save the section where it has pleased Providence to cast my lot, and which I sincerely believe has justice and the Constitution on its side. Having faithfully done my duty to the best of my ability, both to the Union and my section, throughout this agitation, I shall have the consolation, let what will come, that I am free from all responsibility.

DANIEL WEBSTER,

OF MASSACHUSETTS.

(BORN, 1782, DIED, 1852.)

ON THE CONSTITUTION AND THE UNION; SENATE OF THE UNITED STATES, MARCH 7, 1850.

MR. PRESIDENT:

I wish to speak to-day, not as a Massachusetts man, nor as a northern man, but as an American, and a member of the Senate of the United States. It is fortunate that there is a Senate of the United States; a body not yet moved from its propriety, nor lost to a just sense of its own dignity and its own high responsibilities, and a body to which the country looks, with confidence, for wise, moderate, patriotic, and healing counsels. It is not to be denied that we live in the midst of strong agitations and are surrounded by very considerable dangers to our institutions and government. The imprisoned winds are let loose. The East, the North, and the stormy South combine to throw the whole sea into commotion, to toss its billows to the skies, and disclose its profoundest depths. I do not affect to regard myself, Mr. President, as holding, or fit to hold, the helm in this combat with the political elements; but I have a duty to perform, and I mean to perform it with fidelity, not without a sense of existing dangers, but not without hope. I have a part to act, not for my own security or safety, for I am looking out for no fragment upon which to float away from the wreck, if wreck there must be, but for the good of the whole, and the preservation of all; and there is that which will keep me to my duty during this struggle, whether the sun and the stars shall appear for many days. I speak to-day for the preservation of the Union. "Hear me for my cause." I speak to-day out of a solicitous and anxious heart, for the restoration to the country of that quiet and that harmony which make the blessings of this Union so rich, and so dear to us all. These are the topics that I propose to myself to discuss; these are the motives, and the sole motives, that influence me in the wish to communicate my opinions to the Senate and the country; and if I can do any thing, however little, for the promotion of these ends, I shall have accomplished all that I expect.

* * * We all know, sir, that slavery has existed in the world from time immemorial. There was slavery in the earliest periods of history, among the Oriental nations. There was slavery among the Jews; the theocratic government of that people issued no injunction against it. There was slavery among the Greeks. * * * At the introduction of Christianity, the Roman world was full of slaves, and I suppose there is to be found no injunction against that relation between man and man in the teachings of the Gospel of Jesus Christ or of any of his apostles. * * * Now, sir, upon the general nature and influence of slavery there exists a wide difference of opinion between the northern portion of this country and the southern. It is said on the one side, that, although not the subject of any injunction or direct prohibition in the New Testament, slavery is a wrong; that it is founded merely in the right of the strongest; and that it is an oppression, like unjust wars, like all those conflicts by which a powerful nation subjects a weaker to its will; and that, in its nature, whatever may be said of it in the modifications which have taken place, it is not according to the meek spirit of the Gospel. It is not "kindly affectioned"; it does not "seek another's, and not its own"; it does not "let the oppressed go free." These are sentiments that are cherished, and of late with greatly augmented force, among the people of the Northern States. They have taken hold of the religious sentiment of that part of the country, as they have, more or less, taken hold of the religious feelings of a considerable portion of mankind. The South upon the other side, having been accustomed to this relation between the two races all their lives; from their birth, having been taught, in general, to treat the subjects of this bondage with care and kindness, and I believe, in general, feeling great kindness for them, have not taken the view of the subject which I have mentioned. There are thousands of religious men, with consciences as tender as any of their brethren at the North, who do not see the unlawfulness of slavery; and there are more thousands, perhaps, that, whatsoever they may think of it in its origin, and as a matter depending upon natural rights, yet take things as they are, and, finding slavery to be an established relation of the society in which they live, can see no way in which, let their opinions on the abstract question be what they may, it is in the power of this generation to relieve themselves from this relation. And candor obliges me to say, that I believe they are just as conscientious many of them, and the religious people, all of them, as they are at the North who hold different opinions.

There are men who, with clear perceptions, as they think, of their own duty, do not see how too eager a pursuit of one duty may involve them in the violation of others, or how too warm an embracement of one truth may lead to a disregard of other truths just as important. As I heard it stated strongly, not many days ago, these persons are disposed to mount upon some particular duty, as upon a war-horse, and to drive furiously on and upon and over all other duties that may stand in the way. There are men who, in reference to disputes of that sort, are of opinion that human duties may be ascertained with the exactness of mathematics. They deal with morals as with mathematics; and they think what is right may be distinguished from what is wrong with the precision of an algebraic equation. They have, therefore, none too much charity toward others who differ from them. They are apt, too, to think that nothing is good but what is perfect, and that there are no compromises or modifications to be made in consideration of difference of opinion or in deference to other men's judgment. If their perspicacious vision enables them to detect a spot on the face of the sun, they think that a good reason why the sun should be struck down from heaven. They prefer the chance of running into utter darkness to living in heavenly light, if that heavenly light be not absolutely without any imperfection. * * *

But we must view things as they are. Slavery does exist in the United States. It did exist in the States before the adoption of this Constitution, and at that time. Let us, therefore, consider for a moment what was the state of sentiment, North and South, in regard to slavery,—in regard to slavery, at the time this Constitution was adopted. A remarkable change has taken place since; but what did the wise and great men of all parts of the country think of slavery then? In what estimation did they hold it at the time when this Constitution was adopted? It will be found, sir, if we will carry ourselves by historical research back to that day, and ascertain men's opinions by authentic records still existing among us, that there was no diversity of opinion between the North and the South upon the subject of slavery. It will be found that both parts of the country held it equally an evil, a moral and political evil. It will not be found that, either at the North or at the South, there was much, though there was some, invective against slavery as inhuman and cruel. The great ground of objection to it was political; that it weakened the social fabric; that, taking the place of free labor, society became less strong and labor less productive; and therefore we find from all the eminent men of the time the clearest expression of their opinion that slavery is an evil. They ascribed its existence here, not without truth, and not without some acerbity of temper and force of language, to the injurious policy of the mother country, who, to favor the navigator, had entailed these evils upon the colonies. * * * You observe, sir, that the term *slave*, or *slavery*, is not used in the Constitution. The Constitution does not require that "fugitive slaves" shall be deliverd up. It requires that persons held to service in one State, and escaping into another, shall be delivered up. Mr. Madison opposed the introduction of the term *slave*, or *slavery*, into the Constitution; for he said, that he did not wish to see it recognized by the Constitution of the United States of America that there could be property in men. * * *

Here we may pause. There was, if not an entire unanimity, a general concurrence of sentiment running through the whole community, and especially entertained by the eminent men of all parts of the country. But soon a change began, at the North and the South, and a difference of opinion showed itself; the North growing much more warm and strong against slavery, and the South growing much more warm and strong in its support. Sir, there is no generation of mankind whose opinions are not subject to be influenced by what appear to them to be their present emergent and exigent interests. I impute to the South no particularly selfish view in the change which has come over her. I impute to her certainly no dishonest view. All that has happened has been natural. It has followed those causes which always influence the human mind and operate upon it. What, then, have been the causes which have created so new a feeling in favor of slavery in the South, which have changed the whole nomenclature of the South on that subject, so that, from being thought and described in the terms I have mentioned and will not repeat, it has now become an institution, a cherished institution, in that quarter; no evil, no scourge, but a great religious, social, and moral blessing, as I think I have heard it latterly spoken of? I suppose this, sir, is owing to the rapid growth and sudden extension of the cotton plantations of the South. So far as any motive consistent with honor, justice, and general judgment could act, it was the cotton interest that gave a new desire to promote slavery, to spread it, and to use its labor. * * *

Mr. President, sometimes when a man is found in a new relation to things around him and to other men, he says the world has changed, and that he is not changed. I believe, sir, that our self-respect leads us often to make this declaration in regard to ourselves when it is not exactly true. An individual is more apt to change, perhaps, than all the world around him. But under the present circumstances, and under the responsibility which I know I incur by what I am now stating here, I feel at liberty to recur to the various expressions and statements, made at various times, of my own opinions and resolutions respecting the admission of Texas, and all that has followed.

* * * On other occasions, in debate here, I have expressed my determination to vote for no acquisition, or cession, or annexation, North or South, East or West. My opinion has been, that we have territory enough, and that we should follow the Spartan maxim : " Improve, adorn what you have,"—seek no further. I think that it was in some observations that I made on the three million loan bill that I avowed this sentiment. In short, sir, it has been avowed quite as often in as many places, and before as many assemblies, as any humble opinions of mine ought to be avowed.

But now that, under certain conditions, Texas is in the Union, with all her territory, as a slave State, with a solemn pledge also that, if she shall be divided into many States, those States may come in as slave States south of 36° 30′, how are we to deal with this subject? I know no way of honest legislation, when the proper time comes for the enactment, but to carry into effect all that we have stipulated to do. * * * That is the meaning of the contract which our friends, the northern Democracy, have left us to fulfil; and I, for one, mean to fulfil it, because I will not violate the faith of the Government. What I mean to say is, that the time for the admission of new States formed out of Texas, the number of such States, their boundaries, the requisite amount of population, and all other things connected with the admission, are in the free discretion of Congress, except this: to wit, that when new States formed out of Texas are to be admitted, they have a right, by legal stipulation and contract, to come in as slave States.

Now, as to California and New Mexico, I hold slavery to be excluded from these territories by a law even superior to that which admits and sanctions it in Texas. I mean the law of nature, of physical geography, the law of the formation of the earth. That law settles forever, with a strength beyond all terms of human enactment, that slavery cannot exist in California or New Mexico. Understand me, sir; I mean slavery as we regard it; the slavery of the colored race as it exists in the southern States. I shall not discuss the point, but leave it to the learned gentlemen who have undertaken to discuss it; but I suppose there is no slavery of that description in California now. I understand that *peonism*, a sort of penal servitude, exists there, or rather a sort of voluntary sale of a man and his offspring for debt, an arrangement of a peculiar nature known to the law of Mexico. But what I mean to say is, that it is impossible that African slavery, as we see it among us, should find its way, or be introduced, into California and New Mexico, as any other natural impossibility. California and New Mexico are Asiatic in their formation and scenery. They are composed of vast ridges of mountains of great height, with broken ridges and deep valleys. The sides of these mountains are entirely barren; their tops capped by perennial snow. There may be in California, now made free by its constitution, and no doubt there are, some tracts of valuable land. But it is not so in New Mexico. Pray, what is the evidence which every gentleman must have obtained on this subject, from information sought by himself or communicated by others? I have inquired and read all I could find, in order to acquire information on this important subject. What is there in New Mexico that could, by any possibility, induce anybody to go there with slaves! There are some narrow strips of tillable land on the borders of the rivers; but the rivers themselves dry up before midsummer is gone. All that the people can do in that region is to raise some little articles, some little wheat for their *tortillas*, and that by irrigation. And who expects to see a hundred black men cultivating tobacco, corn, cotton, rice, or any thing else, on lands in New Mexico, made fertile by irrigation?

I look upon it, therefore, as a fixed fact, to use the current expression of the day, that both California and New Mexico are destined to be free, so far as they are settled at all, which I believe, in regard to New Mexico, will be but partially, for a great length of time; free by the arrangement of things ordained by the Power above us. I have therefore to say, in this respect also, that this country is fixed for freedom, to as many persons as shall ever live in it, by a less repealable law than that which attaches to the right of holding slaves in Texas; and I will say further, that, if a resolution or a bill were now before us, to provide a territorial government for New Mexico, I would not vote to put any prohibition into it whatever. Such a prohibition would be idle, as it respects any effect it would have upon the territory; and I would not take pains uselessly to reaffirm an ordinance of nature, nor to re-enact the will of God. I would put in no Wilmot proviso for the mere purpose of a taunt or a reproach. I would put into it no evidence of the votes of superior power, exercised for no purpose but to wound the pride, whether a just and a rational pride, or an irrational pride, of the citizens of the southern States. I have no such object, no such purpose. They would think it a taunt, an indignity; they would think it to be an act taking away from them what they regard as a proper equality of privilege. Whether they expect to realize any benefit from it or not, they would think it at least a plain theoretic wrong; that something more or less derogatory to their character and their rights had taken place. I propose to inflict no such wound upon anybody, unless something essentially important to the country, and efficient to the preservation of liberty and freedom, is to be effected. I repeat, therefore, sir, and, as I do not propose to address the Senate often on this subject, I repeat it because I wish it to be distinctly understood, that, for the reasons stated, if a proposition were now here to establish a government for New Mexico, and it was moved to insert a provision for a prohibition of slavery, I would not vote for it. * * * Sir, we hear occasionally of the annexation of Canada; and if there be any man, any of the northern Democracy, or any of the Free Soil party, who supposes it necessary to insert a Wilmot Proviso in a territorial government for New Mexico, that man would, of course, be of opinion that it is necessary to protect the everlasting snows of Canada from the foot of slavery by the same overspreading wing of an act of Congress. Sir, wherever there is a substantive good to be done, wherever there is a foot of land to be prevented from becoming slave territory, I am ready to assert the principle of the exclusion of slavery. I am pledged to it from the year 1837; I have been pledged to it again and again; and I will perform these pledges; but I will not do a thing unnecessarily that wounds the feelings of others, or that does discredit to my own understanding. * * *

Mr. President, in the excited times in which we live, there is found to exist a state of crimination and recrimination between the North and South. There are lists of grievances produced by each; and those grievances, real or supposed, alienate the minds of one portion of the country from the other, exasperate the feelings, and subdue the sense of fraternal affection, patriotic love, and mutual regard. I shall bestow a little attention, sir, upon these various grievances existing on the one side and on the other. I begin with complaints of the South. I will not answer, further than I have, the general statements of the honorable Senator from South Carolina, that the North has prospered at the expense of the South in consequence of the manner of administering this Government, in the collection of its revenues, and so forth. These are disputed topics, and I have no inclination to enter into them. But I will allude to other complaints of the South, and especially to one which has in my opinion, just foundation; and that is, that there has been found at the North, among individuals and among legislators, a disinclination to perform fully their constitutional duties in regard to the return of persons bound to service who have escaped into the free States. In that respect, the South, in my judgment, is right, and the North is wrong. Every member of every Northern legislature is bound by oath, like every other officer in the country, to support the Constitution of the United States; and the article of the Constitution which says to these States that they shall deliver up fugitives from service, is as binding in honor and conscience as any other article. No man fulfils his duty in any legislature who sets himself to find excuses, evasions, escapes from this constitutional obligation. I have always thought that the Constitution addressed itself to the legislatures of the States or to the States themselves. It says that those persons escaping to other States "shall be delivered up," and I confess I have always been of the opinion that it was an injunction upon the States themselves. When it is said that a person escaping into another State, and coming therefore within the jurisdiction of that State, shall be delivered up, it seems to me the import of the clause is, that the State itself, in obedience to the Constitution, shall cause him to be delivered up. That is my judgment. I have always entertained that opinion, and I entertain it now. But when the subject, some years ago, was before the Supreme Court of the United States, the majority of the judges held that the power to cause fugitives from service to be delivered up was a power to be exercised under the authority of this Government, I do not know, on the whole, that it may not have been a fortunate decision. My habit is to respect the result of judicial deliberations and the solemnity of judicial decisions. As it now stands, the business of seeing that these fugitives are delivered up resides in the power of Congress and the national judicature, and my friend at the head of the Judiciary Committee has a bill on the subject now before the Senate, which, with some amendments to it, I propose to support, with all its provisions, to the fullest extent. And I desire to call the attention of all sober-minded men at the North, of all conscientious men, of all men who are not carried away by some fanatical idea or some false impression, to their constitutional obligations. I put it to all the sober and sound minds at the North as a question of morals and a question of conscience. What right have they, in their legislative capacity, or any other capacity, to endeavor to get round this Constitution, or to embarrass the free exercise of the rights secured by the Constitution, to the person whose slaves escape from them? None at all; none at all. Neither in the forum of conscience, nor before the face of the Constitution, are they, in my opinion, justified in such an attempt. Of course it is a matter for their consideration. They probably, in the excitement of the times, have not stopped to consider this. They have followed what seemed to be the current of thought and of motives, as the occasion arose, and they have neglected to investigate fully the real question, and to consider their constitutional obligations; which, I am sure, if they did consider, they would fulfil with alacrity. I repeat, therefore, sir, that here is a well-founded ground of complaint against the North, which ought to be removed, which is now in the power of the different departments of this government to remove; which calls for the enactment of proper laws authorizing the judicature of this Government, in the several States, to do all that is necessary for the recapture of fugitive slaves and for their restoration to those who claim them. Wherever I go, and whenever I speak on the subject, and when I speak here I desire to speak to the whole North, I say that the South has been injured in this respect, and has a right to complain; and the North has been too careless of what I think the Constitution peremptorily and emphatically enjoins upon her as a duty.

Complaint has been made against certain resolutions that emanate from legislatures at the North, and are sent here to us, not only on the subject of slavery in this District, but sometimes recommending Congress to consider the means of abolishing slavery in the States. I should be sorry to be called upon to present any resolutions here which could not be referable to any committee or any power in Congress; and therefore I should be unwilling to receive from the legislature of Massachusetts any instructions to present resolutions expressive of any opinion whatever on the subject of slavery, as it exists at the present moment in the States, for two reasons: because I do not consider that I, as her representative here, have any thing to do with it. It has become, in my opinion, quite too common; and if the legislatures of the States do not like that opinion, they have a great deal more power to put it down than I have to uphold it; it has become, in my opinion, quite too common a practice for the State legislatures to present resolutions here on all subjects and to instruct us on all subjects. There is no public man that requires instruction more than I do, or who requires information more than I do, or desires it more heartily; but I do not like to have it in too imperative a shape. * * *

Then, sir, there are the Abolition societies, of which I am unwilling to speak, but in regard to which I have very clear notions and opinions. I do not think them useful. I think their operations for the last twenty years have produced nothing good or valuable. At the same time, I believe thousands of their members to be honest and good men, perfectly well-meaning men. They have excited feelings; they think they must do something for the cause of liberty; and, in their sphere of action, they do not see what else they can do than to contribute to an abolition press, or an abolition society, or to pay an abolition lecturer. I do not mean to impute gross motives even to the leaders of these societies, but I am not blind to the consequences of their proceedings. I cannot but see what mischief their interference with the South has produced. And is it not plain to every man? Let any gentleman who entertains doubts on this point, recur to the debates in the Virginia House of Delegates in 1832, and he will see with what freedom a proposition made by Mr. Jefferson Randolph, for the gradual abolition of slavery was discussed in that body. Every one spoke of slavery as he thought; very ignominous and disparaging names and epithets were applied to it. The debates in the House of Delegates on that occasion, I believe were all published. They were read by every colored man who could read, and to those who could not read, those debates were read by others. At that time Virginia was not unwilling or afraid to discuss this question, and to let that part of her population know as much of the discussion as they could learn. That was in 1832. As has been said by the honorable member from South Carolina, these abolition societies commenced their course of action in 1835. It is said, I do not know how true it may be, that they sent incendiary publications into the slave States; at any rate, they attempted to arouse, and did arouse, a very strong feeling; in other words, they created great agitation in the North against Southern slavery. Well, what was the result? The bonds of the slaves were bound more firmly than before, their rivets were more strongly fastened. Public opinion, which in Virginia had begun to be exhibited against slavery, and was opening out for the discussion of the question, drew back and shut itself up in its castle. I wish to know whether anybody in Virginia can now talk openly, as Mr. Randolph, Governor McDowel, and others talked in 1832, and sent their remarks to the press? We all know the fact, and we all know the cause; and every thing that these agitating people have done has been, not to enlarge, but to restrain, not to set free, but to bind faster, the slave population of the South. * * *

There are also complaints of the North against the South. I need not go over them particularly. The first and gravest is, that the North adopted the Constitution, recognizing the existence of slavery in the States, and recognizing the right, to a certain extent, of the representation of slaves in Congress, under a state of sentiment and expectation which does not now exist; and that by events, by circumstances, by the eagerness of the South to acquire territory and extend her slave population, the North finds itself, in regard to the relative influence of the South and the North, of the free States and the slave States, where it never did expect to find itself when they agreed to the compact of the Constitution. They complain, therefore, that, instead of slavery being regarded as an evil, as it was then, an evil which all hoped would be extinguished gradually, it is now regarded by the South as an institution to be cherished, and preserved, and extended; an institution which the South has already extended to the utmost of her power by the acquisition of new territory.

Well, then, passing from that, everybody in the North reads; and everybody reads whatsoever the newspapers contain; and the newspapers, some of them, especially those presses to which I have alluded, are careful to spread about among the people every reproachful sentiment uttered by any Southern man bearing at all against the North; every thing that is calculated to exasperate and to alienate; and there are many such things, as everybody will admit, from the South, or from portions of it, which are disseminated among the reading people; and they do exasperate, and alienate, and produce a most mischievous effect upon the public mind at the North. Sir, I would not notice things of this sort appearing in obscure quarters; but one thing has occurred in this debate which struck me very forcibly. An honorable member from Louisiana addressed us the other day on this subject. I suppose there is not a more amiable and worthy gentleman in this chamber, nor a gentleman who would be more slow to give offence to any body, and he did not mean in his remarks to give offence. But what did he say? Why, sir, he took pains to run a contrast between the slaves of the South and the laboring people of the North, giving the preference, in all points of condition, and comfort, and happiness to the slaves of the South. The honorable member, doubtless, did not suppose that he gave any offence, or did any injustice. He was merely expressing his opinion. But does he know how remarks of that sort will be received by the laboring people of the North? Why, who are the laboring people of the North? They are the whole North. They are the people who till their own farms with their own hands; freeholders, educated men, independent men. Let me say, sir, that five sixths of the whole property of the North is in the hands of the laborers of the North; they cultivate their farms, they educate their children, they provide the means of independence. If they are not freeholders, they earn wages; these wages accumulate, are turned into capital, into new freeholds, and small capitalists are created. Such is the case, and such the course of things, among the industrious and frugal. And what can these people think when so respectable and worthy a gentleman as the member from Louisiana undertakes to prove that the absolute ignorance and the abject slavery of the South are more in conformity with the high purposes and destiny of immortal, rational, human beings, than the educated, the independent free labor of the North?

There is a more tangible and irritating cause of grievance at the North. Free blacks are constantly employed in the vessels of the North, generally as cooks or stewards. When the vessel arrives at a southern port, these free colored men are taken on shore, by the police or municipal authority, imprisoned, and kept in prison till the vessel is again ready to sail. This is not only irritating, but exceedingly unjustifiable and oppressive. Mr. Hoar's mission, some time ago to South Carolina, was a well-intended effort to remove this cause of complaint. The North thinks such imprisonments illegal and unconstitutional; and as the cases occur constantly and frequently they regard it as a grievance.

Now, sir, so far as any of these grievances have their foundation in matters of law, they can be redressed, and ought to be redressed; and so far as they have their foundation in matters of opinion, in sentiment, in mutual crimination and recrimination, all that we can do is to endeavor to allay the agitation, and cultivate a better feeling and more fraternal sentiments between the South and the North.

Mr. President, I should much prefer to have heard from every member on this floor declarations of opinion that this Union could never be dissolved, than the declaration of opinion by anybody, that in any case, under the pressure of any circumstances, such a dissolution was possible. I hear with distress and anguish the word "secession," especially when it falls from the lips of those who are patriotic, and known to the country, and known all over the world for their political services. Secession! Peaceable secession! Sir, your eyes and mine are never destined to see that miracle. The dismemberment of this vast country without convulsion! The breaking up of the fountains of the great deep without ruffling the surface! Who is so foolish—I beg everybody's pardon—as to expect to see any such thing? Sir, he who sees these States, now revolving in harmony around a common centre, and expects to see them quit their places and fly off without convulsion, may look the next hour to see the heavenly bodies rush from their spheres, and jostle against each other in the realms of space, without causing the wreck of the universe. There can be no such thing as a peaceable secession. Peaceable secession is an utter impossibility. Is the great Constitution under which we live, covering this whole country, is it to be thawed and melted away by secession, as the snows on the mountain melt under the influence of a vernal sun, disappear almost unobserved, and run off? No, sir! No, sir! I will not state what might produce the disruption of the Union; but, sir, I see as plainly as I can see the sun in heaven what that disruption itself must produce; I see that it must produce war, and such a war as I will not describe, *in its twofold character*.

Peaceable secession! Peaceable secession! The concurrent agreement of all the members of this great Republic to separate! A voluntary separation, with alimony on one side and on the other. Why, what would be the result? Where is the line to be drawn? What States are to secede? What is to remain American? What am I to be? An American no longer? Am I to become a sectional man, a local man, a separatist, with no country in common with the gentlemen who sit around me here, or who fill the other house of Congress? Heaven forbid! Where is the flag of the Republic to remain? Where is the eagle still to tower? or is he to cower, and shrink, and fall to the ground? Why, sir, our ancestors, our fathers and our grandfathers, those of them that are yet living amongst us with prolonged lives, would rebuke and reproach us; and our children and our grandchildren would cry out shame upon us, if we of this generation should dishonor these ensigns of the power of the Government and the harmony of that Union which is every day felt among us with so much joy and gratitude. What is to become of the army? What is to become of the navy? What is to become of the public lands? How is each of the thirty States to defend itself? I know, although the idea has not been stated distinctly, there is to be, or it is supposed possible that there will be, a Southern Confederacy. I do not mean, when I allude to this statement, that any one seriously contemplates such a state of things. I do not mean to say that it is true, but I have heard it suggested elsewhere, that the idea has been entertained, that, after the dissolution of this Union, a Southern Confederacy might be formed. I am sorry, sir, that it has ever been thought of, talked of, in the wildest flights of human imagination. But the idea, so far as it exists, must be of a separation, assigning the slave States to one side, and the free States to the other. Sir, I may express myself too strongly, perhaps, but there are impossibilities in the natural as well as in the physical world, and I hold the idea of the separation of these States, those that are free to form one government, and those that are slave-holding to form another, as such an impossibility. We could not separate the States by any such line, if we were to draw it. We could not sit down here to-day and draw a line of separation that would satisfy any five men in the country. There are natural causes that would keep and tie us together, and there are social and domestic relations which we could not break if we would, and which we should not if we could.

Sir, nobody can look over the face of this country at the present moment, nobody can see where its population is the most dense and growing, without being ready to admit, and compelled to admit, that erelong the strength of America will be in the Valley of the Mississippi. Well, now, sir, I beg to inquire what the wildest enthusiast has to say on the possibility of cutting that river in two, and leaving free States at its source and on its branches, and slave States down near its mouth, each forming a separate government? Pray, sir, let me say to the people of this country, that these things are worthy of their pondering and of their consideration. Here, sir, are five millions of freemen in the free States north of the river Ohio. Can anybody suppose that this population can be severed, by a line that divides them from the territory of a foreign and alien government, down somewhere, the Lord knows where, upon the lower banks of the Mississippi? What would become of Missouri? Will she join the *arrondissement* of the slave States? Shall the man from the Yellowstone and the Platte be connected, in the new republic, with the man who lives on the southern extremity of the Cape of Florida? Sir, I am ashamed to pursue this line of remark. I dislike it, I have an utter disgust for it. I would rather hear of natural blasts and mildews, war, pestilence, and famine, than to hear gentlemen talk of secession. To break up this great Government! to dismember this glorious country! to astonish Europe with an act of folly such as Europe for two centuries has never beheld in any government or any people! No, sir! no, sir! There will be no secession! Gentlemen are not serious when they talk of secession.

Sir, I hear there is to be a convention held at Nashville. I am bound to believe that if worthy gentlemen meet at Nashville in convention, their object will be to adopt conciliatory counsels; to advise the South to forbearance and moderation, and to advise the North to forbearance and moderation; and to inculcate principles of brotherly love and affection, and attachment to the Constitution of the country as it now is. I believe, if the convention meet at all, it will be for this purpose; for certainly, if they meet for any purpose hostile to the Union, they have been singularly inappropriate in their selection of a place. I remember, sir, that, when the treaty of Amiens was concluded between France and England, a sturdy Englishman and a distinguished orator, who regarded the conditions of the peace as ignominious to England, said in the House of Commons, that if King William could know the terms of that treaty, he would turn in his coffin! Let me commend this saying to Mr. Windham, in all its emphasis and in all its force, to any persons who shall meet at Nashville for the purpose of concerting measures for the overthrow of this Union over the bones of Andrew Jackson. * * *

And now, Mr. President, instead of speaking of the possibility or utility of secession, instead of dwelling in those caverns of darkness, instead of groping with those ideas so full of all that is horrid and horrible, let us come out into the light of the day; let us enjoy the fresh air of Liberty and Union; let us cherish those hopes which belong to us; let us devote ourselves to those great objects that are fit for our consideration and our action; let us raise our conceptions to the magnitude and the importance of the duties that devolve upon us; let our comprehension be as broad as the country for which we act, our aspirations as high as its certain destiny; let us not be pigmies in a case that calls for men. Never did there devolve on any generation of men higher trusts than now devolve upon us, for the preservation of this Constitution and the harmony and peace of all who are destined to live under it. Let us make our generation one of the strongest and brightest links in that golden chain which is destined, I fondly believe, to grapple the people of all the States to this Constitution for ages to come. We have a great, popular, Constitutional Government, guarded by law and by judicature, and defended by the affections of the whole people. No monarchical throne presses these States together, no iron chain of military power encircles them; they live and stand under a Government popular in its form, representative in its character, founded upon principles of equality, and so constructed, we hope, as to last forever. In all its history it has been beneficent; it has trodden down no man's liberty; it has crushed no State. Its daily respiration is liberty and patriotism; its yet youthful veins are full of enterprise, courage, and honorable love of glory and renown. Large before, the country has now, by recent events, become vastly larger. This Republic now extends, with a vast breadth across the whole continent. The two great seas of the world wash the one and the other shore. We realize, on a mighty scale, the beautiful description of the ornamental border of the buckler of Achilles:

> " Now, the broad shield complete, the artist crowned
> With his last hand, and poured the ocean round;
> In living silver seemed the waves to roll,
> And beat the buckler's verge, and bound the whole."

HENRY CLAY,

OF KENTUCKY.

(BORN 1777, DIED 1852.)

ON THE COMPROMISE OF 1850; UNITED STATES SENATE, JULY 22, 1850.

MR. PRESIDENT:

In the progress of this debate it has been again and again argued that perfect tranquillity reigns throughout the country, and that there is no disturbance threatening its peace, endangering its safety, but that which was produced by busy, restless politicians. It has been maintained that the surface of the public mind is perfectly smooth and undisturbed by a single billow. I most heartily wish I could concur in this picture of general tranquillity that has been drawn upon both sides of the Senate. I am no alarmist; nor, I thank God, at the advanced age at which His providence has been pleased to allow me to reach, am I very easily alarmed by any human event; but I totally misread the signs of the times, if there be that state of profound peace and quiet, that absence of all just cause of apprehension of future danger to this confederacy, which appears to be entertained by some other senators. Mr. President, all the tendencies of the times, I lament to say, are toward disquietude, if not more fatal consequences. When before, in the midst of profound peace with all the nations of the earth, have we seen a convention, representing a considerable portion of one great part of the Republic, meet to deliberate about measures of future safety in connection with great interests of that quarter of the country? When before have we seen, not one, but more—some half a dozen legislative bodies solemnly resolving that if any one of these measures—the admission of California, the adoption of the Wilmot proviso, the abolition of slavery in the District of Columbia—should be adopted by Congress, measures of an extreme character, for the safety of the great interests to which I refer, in a particular section of the country, would be resorted to? For years, this subject of the abolition of slavery, even within this District of Columbia, small as is the number of slaves here, has been a source of constant irritation and disquiet. So of the subject of the recovery of fugitive slaves who have escaped from their lawful owners: not a mere border contest, as has been supposed—although there, undoubtedly, it has given rise to more irritation than in other portions of the Union—but everywhere throughout the slave-holding country it has been felt as a great evil, a great wrong which required the intervention of congressional power. But these two subjects, unpleasant as has been the agitation to which they have given rise, are nothing in comparison to those which have sprung out of the acquisitions recently made from the Republic of Mexico. These are not only great and leading causes of just apprehension as respects the future, but all the minor circumstances of the day intimate danger ahead, whatever may be its final issue and consequence.

Mr. President, I will not dwell upon other concomitant causes, all having the same tendency, and all well calculated to awaken, to arouse us—if, as I hope the fact is, we are all of us sincerely desirous of preserving this Union—to rouse us to dangers which really exist, without underrating them upon the one hand, or magnifying them upon the other. * * *

It has been objected against this measure

that it is a compromise. It has been said that it is a compromise of principle, or of a principle. Mr. President, what is a compromise? It is a work of mutual concession—an agreement in which there are reciprocal stipulations—a work in which, for the sake of peace and concord, one party abates his extreme demands in consideration of an abatement of extreme demands by the other party: it is a measure of mutual concession—a measure of mutual sacrifice. Undoubtedly, Mr. President, in all such measures of compromise, one party would be very glad to get what he wants, and reject what he does not desire, but which the other party wants. But when he comes to reflect that, from the nature of the Government and its operations, and from those with whom he is dealing, it is necessary upon his part, in order to secure what he wants, to grant something to the other side, he should be reconciled to the concession which he has made, in consequence of the concession which he is to receive, if there is no great principle involved, such as a violation of the Constitution of the United States. I admit that such a compromise as that ought never to be sanctioned or adopted. But I now call upon any senator in his place to point out from the beginning to the end, from California to New Mexico, a solitary provision in this bill which is violative of the Constitution of the United States.

Sir, adjustments in the shape of compromise may be made without producing any such consequences as have been apprehended. There may be a mutual forbearance. You forbear on your side to insist upon the application of the restriction denominated the Wilmot proviso. Is there any violation of principle there? The most that can be said, even assuming the power to pass the Wilmot proviso, which is denied, is that there is a forbearance to exercise, not a violation of, the power to pass the proviso. So, upon the other hand, if there was a power in the Constitution of the United States authorizing the establishment of slavery in any of the Territories—a power, however, which is controverted by a large portion of this Senate—if there was a power under the Constitution to establish slavery, the forbearance to exercise that power is no violation of the Constitution, any more than the Constitution is violated by a forbearance to exercise numerous powers, that might be specified, that are granted in the Constitution, and that remain dormant until they come to be exercised by the proper legislative authorities. It is said that the bill presents the state of coercion—that members are coerced, in order to get what they want, to vote for that which they disapprove. Why, sir, what coercion is there? * * * Can it be said upon the part of our Northern friends, because they have not got the Wilmot proviso incorporated in the territorial part of the bill, that they are coerced—wanting California, as they do, so much—to vote for the bill, if they do vote for it? Sir, they might have imitated the noble example of my friend (Senator Cooper, of Pennsylvania), from that State upon whose devotion to this Union I place one of my greatest reliances for its preservation. What was the course of my friend upon this subject of the Wilmot proviso? He voted for it; and he could go back to his constituents and say, as all of you could go back and say to your constituents, if you chose to do so—"We wanted the Wilmot proviso in the bill; we tried to get it in; but the majority of the Senate was against it." The question then came up whether we should lose California, which has got an interdiction in her constitution, which, in point of value and duration, is worth a thousand Wilmot provisos; we were induced, as my honorable friend would say, to take the bill and the whole of it together, although we were disappointed in our votes with respect to the Wilmot proviso—to take it, whatever omissions may have been made, on account of the superior amount of good it contains. * * *

Not the reception of the treaty of peace negotiated at Ghent, nor any other event which has occurred during my progress in public life, ever gave such unbounded and universal satisfaction as the settlement of the Missouri compromise. We may argue from like causes like effects. Then, indeed, there was great excitement. Then, indeed, all the legislatures of the North called out for the exclusion of Missouri, and all the legislatures of the South called out for her admission as a State. Then, as now, the country was agitated like the ocean in the midst of a turbulent storm. But now, more than then, has this agitation been increased. Now, more than then, are the dangers which exist, if the controversy remains unsettled, more aggravated and more to be dreaded. The idea of disunion was then scarcely a low whisper. Now, it has become a familar language in certain portions of the country. The public mind and the public heart are becoming familiarized with that most dangerous and fatal of all events—the disunion of the States. People begin to contend that this is not so bad a thing as they had supposed. Like the progress in all human affairs, as we approach danger it disappears, it diminishes in our conception, and we no longer regard it with that awful apprehension of consequences that we did before we came into contact with it. Everywhere now there is a state of things, a degree of alarm and apprehension, and determination to fight, as they regard it, against the aggressions of the North. That did not so demonstrate itself at the period of the Missouri compromise. It was followed, in consequence of the adoption of the measure which settled the difficulty of Missouri, by peace, harmony, and tranquillity. So, now, I infer, from the greater amount of agitation, from the greater amount of danger, that, if you adopt the measures under consideration, they, too, will be followed by the same amount of contentment, satisfaction, peace, and tranquillity, which ensued after the Missouri compromise. * * *

The responsibility of this great measure passes from the hands of the committee, and from my hands. They know, and I know, that it is an awful and tremendous responsibility. I hope that you will meet it with a just conception and a true appreciation of its magnitude, and the magnitude of the consequences that may ensue from your decision one way or the other. The alternatives, I fear, which the measure presents, are concord and increased discord; a servile civil war, originating in its causes on the lower Rio Grande, and terminating possibly in its consequences on the upper Rio Grande in the Santa Fé country, or the restoration of harmony and fraternal kindness. I believe from the bottom of my soul, that the measure is the reunion of this Union. I believe it is the dove of peace, which, taking its aërial flight from the dome of the Capitol, carries the glad tidings of assured peace and restored harmony to all the remotest extremities of this distracted land. I believe that it will be attended with all these beneficent effects. And now let us discard all resentment, all passions, all petty jealousies, all personal desires, all love of place, all hankerings after the gilded crumbs which fall from the table of power. Let us forget popular fears, from whatever quarter they may spring. Let us go to the limpid fountain of unadulterated patriotism, and, performing a solemn lustration, return divested of all selfish, sinister, and sordid impurities, and think alone of our God, our country, our consciences, and our glorious Union—that Union without which we shall be torn into hostile fragments, and sooner or later become the victims of military despotism, or foreign domination.

Mr. President, what is an individual man? An atom, almost invisible without a magnifying glass—a mere speck upon the surface of the immense universe; not a second in time, compared to immeasurable, never-beginning, and never-ending eternity; a drop of water in the great deep, which evaporates and is borne off by the winds; a grain of sand, which is soon gathered to the dust from which it sprung. Shall a being so small, so petty, so fleeting, so evanescent, oppose itself to the onward march of a great nation, which is to subsist for ages and ages to come; oppose itself to that long line of posterity which, issuing from our loins, will endure during the existence of the world? Forbid it, God. Let us look to our country and our cause, elevate ourselves to the dignity of pure and disinterested patriots, and save our country from all impending dangers. What if, in the march of this nation to greatness and power, we should be buried beneath the wheels that propel it onward! What are we—what is any man—worth who is not ready and willing to sacrifice himself for the benefit of his country when it is necessary? * * *

If this Union shall become separated, new unions, new confederacies will arise. And with respect to this, if there be any—I hope there is no one in the Senate—before whose imagination is flitting the idea of a great Southern Confederacy to take possession of the Balize and the mouth of the Mississippi, I say in my place never! *never!* NEVER! will we who occupy the broad waters of the Mississippi and its upper tributaries consent that any foreign flag shall float at the Balize or upon the turrets of the Crescent City—NEVER! NEVER! I call upon all the South. Sir, we have had hard words, bitter words, bitter thoughts, unpleasant feelings toward each other in the progress of this great measure. Let us forget them. Let us sacrifice these feelings. Let us go to the altar of our country and swear, as the oath was taken of old, that we will stand by her; that we will support her; that we will uphold her Constitution; that we will preserve her Union; and that we will pass this great, comprehensive, and healing system of measures, which will hush all the jarring elements, and bring peace and tranquillity to our homes.

Let me, Mr. President, in conclusion, say that the most disastrous consequences would occur, in my opinion, were we to go home, doing nothing to satisfy and tranquillize the country upon these great questions. What will be the judgment of mankind, what the judgment of that portion of mankind who are looking upon the progress of this scheme of self-government as being that which holds the highest hopes and expectations of ameliorating the condition of mankind—what will their judgment be? Will not all the monarchs of the Old World pronounce our glorious Republic a disgraceful failure? What will be the judgment of our constituents, when we return to them and they ask us: "How have you left your country? Is all quiet—all happy? Are all the seeds of distraction or division crushed and dissipated?" And, sir, when you come into the bosom of your family, when you come to converse with the partner of your fortunes, of your happiness, and of your sorrows, and when in the midst of the common offspring of both of you, she asks you: "Is there any danger of civil war? Is there any danger of the torch being applied to any portion of the country? Have you settled the questions which you have been so long discussing and deliberating upon at Washington? Is all peace and all quiet?" what response, Mr. President, can you make to that wife of your choice and those children with whom you have been blessed by God? Will you go home and leave all in disorder and confusion—all unsettled—all open? The contentions and agitations of the past will be increased and augmented by the agitations resulting from our neglect to decide them. Sir, we shall stand condemned by all human judgment below, and of that above it is not for me to speak. We shall stand condemned in our own consciences, by our own constituents, and by our own country. The measure may be defeated. I have been aware that its passage for many days was not absolutely certain. From the first to the last, I hoped and believed it would pass, because from the first to the last I believed it was founded on the principles of just and righteous concession of mutual conciliation. I believe that it deals unjustly by no part of the Republic; that it saves their honor, and, as far as it is dependent upon Congress, saves the interests of all quarters of the country. But, sir, I have known that the decision of its fate depended upon four or five votes in the Senate of the United States, whose ultimate judgment we could not count upon the one side or the other with absolute certainty. Its fate is now committed to the Senate, and to those five or six votes to which I have referred. It may be defeated. It is possible that, for the chastisement of our sins and transgressions, the rod of Providence may be still applied to us, may be still suspended over us. But, if defeated, it will be a triumph of ultraism and impracticability—a triumph of a most extraordinary conjunction of extremes; a victory won by abolitionism; a victory achieved by freesoilism; a victory of discord and agitation over peace and tranquillity; and I pray to Almighty God that it may not, in consequence of the inauspicious result, lead to the most unhappy and disastrous consequences to our beloved country.

MR. BARNWELL:—It is not my intention to reply to the argument of the Senator from Kentucky, but there were expressions used by him not a little disrespectful to a friend whom I hold very dear. * * * It is true that his political opinions differ very widely from those of the Senator from Kentucky. It may be true, that he, with many great statesmen, may believe that the Wilmot proviso is a grievance to be resisted " to the utmost extremity " by those whose rights it destroys and whose honor it degrades. It is true that he may believe * * * that the admission of California will be the passing of the Wilmot proviso, when we here in Congress give vitality to an act otherwise totally dead, and by our legislation exclude slaveholders from that whole broad territory on the Pacific; and, entertaining this opinion, he may have declared that the contingency will then have occurred which will, in the judgment of most of the slave-holding States, as expressed by their resolutions, justify resistance as to an intolerable aggression. If he does entertain and has expressed such sentiments, he is not to be held up as peculiarly a disunionist. Allow me to say, in reference to this matter, I regret that you have brought it about, but it is true that this epithet " disunionist " is likely soon to have very little terror in it in the South. Words do not make things. " Rebel " was designed as a very odious term when applied by those who would have trampled on the rights of our ancestors, but I believe that the expression became not an ungrateful one to the ears of those who resisted them. It was not the lowest term of abuse to call those who were conscious that they were struggling against oppression; and let me assure gentlemen that the term disunionist is rapidly assuming at the South the meaning which rebel took when it was baptized in the blood of Warren at Bunker Hill, and illustrated by the gallantry of Jasper at Fort Moultrie. * * *

MR. CLAY:—Mr. President, I said nothing with respect to the character of Mr. Rhett, for I might as well name him. I know him personally, and have some respect for him. But, if he pronounced the sentiment attributed to him —of raising the standard of disunion and of resistance to the common government, whatever he has been, if he follows up that declaration by corresponding overt acts, he will be a *traitor*, and I hope he will meet the fate of a traitor.

THE PRESIDENT:—The Chair will be under the necessity of ordering the gallery to be cleared if there is again the slightest interruption. He has once already given warning that he is under the necessity of keeping order. The Senate chamber is not a theatre.

MR. CLAY:—Mr. President, I have heard with pain and regret a confirmation of the remark I made, that the sentiment of disunion is becoming familiar. I hope it is confined to South Carolina. I do not regard as my duty what the honorable Senator seems to regard as his. If Kentucky to-morrow unfurls the banner of resistance unjustly, I never will fight under that banner. I owe a paramount allegiance to the whole Union—a subordinate one to my own State. When my State is right—when it has a cause for resistance—when tyranny, and wrong, and oppression insufferable arise, I will then share her fortunes; but if she summons me to the battle-field, or to support her in any cause which is unjust, against the Union, never, *never* will I engage with her in such cause.

WENDELL PHILLIPS,

OF MASSACHUSETTS.

(BORN 1811, DIED 1884.)

ON THE PHILOSOPHY OF THE ABOLITION MOVEMENT, BEFORE THE MASSACHUSETTS ANTI-SLAVERY SOCIETY, AT BOSTON, JANUARY 27, 1853.

Mr. CHAIRMAN:

I have to present, from the business committee, the following resolution:

Resolved; That the object of this society is now, as it has always been, to convince our countrymen, by arguments addressed to their hearts and consciences, that slave-holding is a heinous crime, and that the duty, safety, and interest of all concerned demand its immediate abolition without expatriation.

I wish, Mr. Chairman, to notice some objections that have been made to our course ever since Mr. Garrison began his career, and which have been lately urged again, with considerable force and emphasis, in the columns of the London *Leader*, the able organ of a very respectable and influential class in England. * * * The charges to which I refer are these: That, in dealing with slave-holders and their apologists, we indulge in fierce denunciations, instead of appealing to their reason and common sense by plain statements and fair argument; that we might have won the sympathies and support of the nation, if we would have submitted to argue this question with a manly patience; but, instead of this, we have outraged the feelings of the community by attacks, unjust and unnecessarily severe, on its most valued institutions, and gratified our spleen by indiscriminate abuse of leading men, who were often honest in their intentions, however mistaken in their views; that we have utterly neglected the ample means that lay around us to convert the nation, submitted to no discipline, formed no plan, been guided by no foresight, but hurried on in childish, reckless, blind, and hot-headed zeal,—bigots in the narrowness of our views, and fanatics in our blind fury of invective and malignant judgment of other men's motives.

There are some who come upon our platform, and give us the aid of names and reputations less burdened than ours with popular odium, who are perpetually urging us to exercise charity in our judgments of those about us, and to consent to argue these questions. These men are ever parading their wish to draw a line between themselves and us, because *they must be permitted* to wait,—to trust more to reason than feeling,—to indulge a generous charity,—to rely on the sure influence of simple truth, uttered in love, etc., etc. I reject with scorn all these implications that *our* judgments are uncharitable,—that *we* are lacking in patience,—that *we* have any other dependence than on the simple truth, spoken with Christian frankness, yet with Christian love. These lectures, to which you, sir, and all of us, have so often listened, would be impertinent, if they were not rather ridiculous for the gross ignorance they betray of the community, of the cause, and of the whole course of its friends.

The article in the *Leader* to which I refer is signed " ION," and may be found in the *Liberator* of December 17, 1852. * * * " Ion" quotes Mr Garrison's original declaration in the *Liberator :* " I am aware that many object to the severity of my language; but is there not cause for severity? I *will* be as harsh as truth and as uncompromising as justice. I am in earnest,—I will not equivocate,—I will not excuse,—I will not retreat a single inch,—AND I WILL BE HEARD. It is *pretended* that I am retarding the cause of emancipation by the coarseness of my invective and the precipitancy of my measures. *The charge is not true.* On this question, my influence, humble as it is, is felt at this moment to a considerable extent, and shall be felt in coming years, not perniciously, but beneficially; not as a curse, but as a blessing; and posterity will bear testimony that I was right. I desire to thank God that He enables me to disregard 'the fear of man which bringeth a snare,' and to speak His truth in its simplicity and power."   *   *   *

"Ion's" charges are the old ones, that we Abolitionists are hurting our own cause; that, instead of waiting for the community to come up to our views, and endeavoring to remove prejudice and enlighten ignorance by patient explanation and fair argument, we fall at once, like children, to abusing every thing and everybody; that we imagine zeal will supply the place of common sense; that we have never shown any sagacity in adapting our means to our ends; have never studied the national character, or attempted to make use of the materials which lay all about us to influence public opinion, but by blind, childish, obstinate fury and indiscriminate denunciation, have become "honestly impotent, and conscientious hinderances."

I claim, before you who know the true state of the case, I claim for the antislavery movement with which this society is identified, that, looking back over its whole course, and considering the men connected with it in the mass, it has been marked by sound judgment, unerring foresight, the most sagacious adaptation of means to ends, the strictest self-discipline, the most thorough research, and an amount of patient and manly argument addressed to the conscience and intellect of the nation, such as no other cause of the kind, in England or this country, has ever offered. I claim, also, that its course has been marked by a cheerful surrender of all individual claims to merit or leadership,—the most cordial welcoming of the slightest effort, of every honest attempt, to lighten or to break the chain of the slave. I need not waste time by repeating the superfluous confession that we are men, and therefore do not claim to be perfect. Neither would I be understood as denying that we use denunciation, and ridicule, and every other weapon that the human mind knows. We must plead guilty, if there be guilt in not knowing how to separate the sin from the sinner. With all the fondness for abstractions attributed to us, we are not yet capable of that. We are fighting a momentous battle at desperate odds,— one against a thousand. Every weapon that ability or ignorance, wit, wealth, prejudice, or fashion can command, is pointed against us. The guns are shotted to their lips. The arrows are poisoned. Fighting against such an array, we cannot afford to confine ourselves to any one weapon. The cause is not ours, so that we might, rightfully, postpone or put in peril the victory by moderating our demands, stifling our convictions, or filing down our rebukes, to gratify any sickly taste of our own, or to spare the delicate nerves of our neighbor. Our clients are three millions of Christian slaves, standing dumb suppliants at the threshold of the Christian world. They have no voice but ours to utter their complaints, or to demand justice. The press, the pulpit, the wealth, the literature, the prejudices, the political arrangements, the present self-interest of the country, are all against us. God has given us no weapon but the truth, faithfully uttered, and addressed, with the old prophets' directness, to the conscience of the individual sinner. The elements which control public opinion and mould the masses are against us. We can but pick off here and there a man from the triumphant majority. We have facts for those who think, arguments for those who reason; but he who cannot be reasoned out of his prejudices must be laughed out of them; he who cannot be argued out of his selfishness must be shamed out of it by the mirror of his hateful self held up relentlessly before his eyes. We live in a land where every man makes broad his phylactery, inscribing thereon, "All men are created equal,"—"God hath made of one blood all nations of men." It seems to us that in such a land there must be, on this question of slavery, sluggards to be awakened, as well as doubters to be convinced. Many more, we verily believe, of the first than of the last. There are far more dead hearts to be quickened, than confused intellects to be cleared up,—more dumb dogs to be made to speak, than doubting consciences to be enlightened. We have use, then, sometimes, for something beside argument.

What is the denunciation with which we are charged? It is endeavoring, in our faltering human speech, to declare the enormity of the sin of making merchandize of men,—of separating husband and wife,—taking the infant from its mother and selling the daughter to prostitution,—of a professedly Christian nation denying, by statute, the Bible to every sixth man and woman of its population, and making it illegal for "two or three" to meet together, except a white man be present! What is this harsh criticism of motives with which we are charged? It is simply holding the intelligent and deliberate actor responsible for the character and consequences of his acts. Is there any thing inherently wrong in such denunciation of such criticism? This we may claim,— we have never judged a man but out of his own mouth. We have seldom, if ever, held him to account, except for acts of which he and his own friends were proud. All that we ask the world and thoughtful men to note are the principles and deeds on which the American pulpit and American public men plume themselves. We always allow our opponents to paint their own pictures. Our humble duty is to stand by and assure the spectators that what they would take for a knave or a hypocrite is really, in American estimation, a Doctor of Divinity or a Secretary of State.

The South is one great brothel, where half a million of women are flogged to prostitution, or, worse still, are degraded to believe it honorable. The public squares of half our great cities echo to the wail of families torn asunder at the auction-block; no one of our fair rivers that has not closed over the negro seeking in death a refuge from a life too wretched to bear; thousands of fugitives skulk along our highways, afraid to tell their names, and trembling at the sight of a human being; free men are kidnapped in our streets, to be plunged into that hell of slavery; and now and then one, as if by miracle, after long years returns to make men aghast with his tale. The press says, "It is all right"; and the pulpit cries, "Amen." They print the Bible in every tongue in which man utters his prayers; and they get the money to do so by agreeing never to give the book, in the language our mothers taught us, to any negro, free or bond, south of Mason and Dixon's line. The press says, "It is all right"; and the pulpit cries, "Amen." The slave lifts up his imploring eyes, and sees in every face but ours the face of an enemy. Prove to me now that harsh rebuke, indignant denunciation, scathing sarcasm, and pitiless ridicule are wholly and always unjustifiable; else we dare not, in so desperate a case, throw away any weapon which ever broke up the crust of an ignorant prejudice, roused a slumbering conscience, shamed a proud sinner, or changed in any way the conduct of a human being. Our aim is to alter public opinion. Did we live in a market, our talk should be of dollars and cents, and we would seek to prove only that slavery was an unprofitable investment. Were the nation one great, pure church, we would sit down and reason of "righteousness, temperance, and judgment to come." Had slavery fortified itself in a college, we would load our cannons with cold facts, and wing our arrows with arguments. But we happen to live in the world,—the world made up of thought and impulse, of self-conceit and self-interest, of weak men and wicked. To conquer, we must reach all. Our object is not to make every man a Christian or a philosopher, but to induce every one to aid in the abolition of slavery. We expect to accomplish our object long before the nation is made over into saints or elevated into philosophers. To change public opinion, we use the very tools by which it was formed. That is, all such as an honest man may touch.

All this I am not only ready to allow, but I should be ashamed to think of the slave, or to look into the face of my fellow-man, if it were otherwise. It is the only thing which justifies us to our own consciences, and makes us able to say we have done, or at least tried to do, our duty.

So far, however you distrust my philosophy, you will not doubt my statements. That we have denounced and rebuked with unsparing fidelity will not be denied. Have we not also addressed ourselves to that other duty, of arguing our question thoroughly?—of using due discretion and fair sagacity in endeavoring to promote our cause? Yes, we have. Every statement we have made has been doubted. Every principle we have laid down has been denied by overwhelming majorities against us. No one step has ever been gained but by the most laborious research and the most exhausting argument. And no question has ever, since Revolutionary days, been so thoroughly investigated or argued here, as that of slavery. Of that research and that argument, of the whole of it, the old-fashioned, fanatical, crazy Garrisonian antislavery movement has been the author. From this band of men has proceeded every important argument or idea which has been broached on the antislavery question from 1830 to the present time. * * * I recognize, as fully as any one can, the ability of the new laborers. * * * I do not mean, either, to assert that they have in every instance borrowed from our treasury their facts and arguments. Left to themselves, they would probably have looked up the one and originated the other. As a matter of fact, however, they have generally made use of the materials collected to their hands. * * * When once brought fully into the struggle, they have found it necessary to adopt the same means, to rely on the same arguments, to hold up the same men and the same measures to public reprobation, with the same bold rebuke and unsparing invective that we have used. All their conciliatory bearing, their painstaking moderation, their constant and anxious endeavor to draw a broad line between their camp and ours, have been thrown away. Just so far as they have been effective laborers, they have found, as we have, their hands against every man, and every man's hand against them. The most experienced of them are ready to acknowledge that our plan has been wise, our course efficient, and that our unpopularity is no fault of ours, but flows necessarily and unavoidably from our position. "I should suspect," says old Fuller, "that his preaching had no salt in it, if no galled horse did wince." Our friends find, after all, that men do not so much hate us as the truth we utter and the light we bring. They find that the community are not the honest seekers after truth which they fancied, but selfish politicians and sectarian bigots, who shiver, like Alexander's butler, whenever the sun shines on them. Experience has driven these new laborers back to our method. We have no quarrel with them —would not steal one wreath of their laurels. All we claim is, that, if they are to be complimented as prudent, moderate, Christian, sagacious, statesmanlike reformers, we deserve the same praise; for they have done nothing that we, in our measure, did not attempt before.

I claim this, that the cause, in its recent aspect, has put on nothing but timidity. It has taken to itself no new weapons of recent years; it has become more compromising,—that is all! It has become neither more persuasive, more learned, more Christian, more charitable, nor more effective than for the twenty years preceding. Mr. Hale, the head of the Free Soil movement, after a career in the Senate that would do honor to any man,—after a six years' course which entitles him to the respect and confidence of the antislavery public,—can put his name, within the last month, to an appeal from the city of Washington, signed by a Houston and a Cass, for a monument to be raised to Henry Clay! If that be the test of charity and courtesy, we cannot give it to the world. Some of the leaders of the Free Soil party of Massachusetts, after exhausting the whole capacity of our language to paint the treachery of Daniel Webster to the cause of liberty, and the evil they thought he was able and seeking to do,—after that, could feel it in their hearts to parade themselves in the funeral procession got up to do him honor! In this we allow we cannot follow them. The deference which every gentleman owes to the proprieties of social life, that self-respect and regard to consistency which is every man's duty,—these, if no deeper feelings, will ever prevent us from giving such proofs of this newly invented Christian courtesy. We do not play politics, antislavery is no half-jest with us; it is a terrible earnest, with life or death, worse than life or death, on the issue. It is no lawsuit, where it matters not to the good feeling of opposing counsel which way the verdict goes, and where advocates can shake hands after the decision as pleasantly as before. When we think of such a man as Henry Clay, his long life, his mighty influence cast always into the scale against the slave, of that irresistible fascination with which he moulded every one to his will; when we remember that, his conscience acknowledging the justice of our cause, and his heart open on every other side to the gentlest impulses, he could sacrifice so remorselessly his convictions and the welfare of millions to his low ambition; when we think how the slave trembled at the sound of his voice, and that, from a multitude of breaking hearts there went up nothing but gratitude to God when it pleased him to call that great sinner from this world, we cannot find it in our hearts, we could not shape our lips to ask any man to do him honor. No amount of eloquence, no sheen of official position, no loud grief of partisan friends, would ever lead us to ask monuments or walk in fine processions for pirates; and the sectarian zeal or selfish ambition which gives up, deliberately and in full knowledge of the facts, three million of human beings to hopeless ignorance, daily robbery, systematic prostitution, and murder, which the law is neither able nor undertakes to prevent or avenge, is more monstrous, in our eyes, than the love of gold which takes a score of lives with merciful quickness on the high seas. Haynau on the Danube is no more hateful to us than Haynau on the Potomac. Why give mobs to one and monuments to the other.

If these things be necessary to courtesy, I cannot claim that we are courteous. We seek only to be honest men, and speak the same of the dead as of the living. If the grave that hides their bodies could swallow also the evil they have done and the example they leave, we might enjoy at least the luxury of forgetting them. But the evil that men do lives after them, and example acquires tenfold authority when it speaks from the grave. History, also, is to be written. How shall a feeble minority, without weight or influence in the country, with no jury of millions to appeal to, —denounced, vilified, and contemned,—how shall we make way against the overwhelming weight of some colossal reputation, if we do not turn from the idolatrous present, and appeal to the human race? saying to your idols of to-day: " Here we are defeated ; but we will write our judgment with the iron pen of a century to come, and it shall never be forgotten, if we can help it, that you were false in your generation to the claims of the slave!" * * *

We are weak here,—out-talked, out-voted. You load our names with infamy, and shout us down. But our words bide their time. We warn the living that we have terrible memories, and their sins are never to be forgotten. We will gibbet the name of every apostate so black and high that his children's children shall blush to bear it. Yet we bear no malice,—cherish no resentment. We thank God that the love of fame, "that last infirmity of noble minds," is shared by the ignoble. In our necessity, we seize this weapon in the slave's behalf, and teach caution to the living by meting out relentless justice to the dead. * * * These, Mr. Chairman, are the reasons why we take care that "the memory of the wicked shall rot."

I have claimed that the antislavery cause has, from the first, been able and dispassionately argued, every objection candidly examined, and every difficulty or doubt anywhere honestly entertained treated with respect. Let me glance at the literature of the cause, and try not so much, in a brief hour, to prove this assertion, as to point out the sources from which any one may satisfy himself of its truth.

I will begin with certainly the ablest and perhaps the most honest statesman who has ever touched the slave question. Any one who will examine John Quincy Adams' speech on Texas, in 1838, will see that he was only seconding the full and able exposure of the Texas plot, prepared by Benjamin Lundy, to one of whose pamphlets Dr. Channing, in his "Letter to Henry Clay," has confessed his obligation. Every one acquainted with those years will allow that the North owes its earliest knowledge and first awakening on that subject to Mr. Lundy, who made long journeys and devoted years to the investigation. His labors have this attestation, that they quickened the zeal and strengthened the hands of such men as Adams and Channing. I have been told that Mr. Lundy prepared a brief for Mr. Adams, and furnished him the materials for his speech on Texas.

Look next at the right of petition. Long

before any member of Congress had opened his mouth in its defence, the Abolition presses and lecturers had examined and defended the limits of this right with profound historical research and eminent constitutional ability. So thoroughly had the work been done, that all classes of the people had made up their minds about it long before any speaker of eminence had touched it in Congress. The politicians were little aware of this. When Mr. Adams threw himself so gallantly into the breach, it is said he wrote anxiously home to know whether he would be supported in Massachusetts, little aware of the outburst of popular gratitude which the northern breeze was even then bringing him, deep and cordial enough to wipe away the old grudge Massachusetts had borne him so long. Mr. Adams himself was only in favor of receiving the petitions, and advised to refuse their prayer, which was the abolition of slavery in the District of Columbia. He doubted the power of Congress to abolish. His doubts were examined by Mr. William Goodell, in two letters of most acute logic, and of masterly ability. If Mr. Adams still retained his doubts, it is certain at least that he never expressed them afterward. When Mr. Clay paraded the same objections, the whole question of the power of Congress over the District was treated by Theodore D. Weld in the fullest manner, and with the widest research,—indeed, leaving nothing to be added: an argument which Dr. Channing characterized as "demonstration," and pronounced the essay "one of the ablest pamphlets from the American press." No answer was ever attempted. The best proof of its ability is that no one since has presumed to doubt the power. Lawyers and statesmen have tacitly settled down into its full acknowledgment.

The influence of the Colonization Society on the welfare of the colored race was the first question our movement encountered. To the close logic, eloquent appeals, and fully sustained charges of Mr. Garrison's letters on that subject no answer was ever made. Judge Jay followed with a work full and able, establishing every charge by the most patient investigation of facts. It is not too much to say of these two volumes, that they left the Colonization Society hopeless at the North. It dares never show its face before the people, and only lingers in some few nooks of sectarian pride, so secluded from the influence of present ideas as to be almost fossil in their character.

The practical working of the slave system, the slave laws, the treatment of slaves, their food, the duration of their lives, their ignorance and moral condition, and the influence of Southern public opinion on their fate, have been spread out in a detail and with a fulness of evidence which no subject has ever received before in this country. Witness the words of Phelps, Bourne, Rankin, Grimke, the "Antislavery Record," and, above all, that encyclopædia of facts and storehouse of arguments, the "Thousand Witnesses" of Mr. Theodore D. Weld. He also prepared that full and valuable tract for the World's Convention called "Slavery and the Internal Slave-Trade in the United States," published in London in 1841. Unique in antislavery literature is Mrs. Child's "Appeal," one of the ablest of our weapons, and one of the finest efforts of her rare genius.

The *Princeton Review*, I believe, first challenged the Abolitionists to an investigation of the teachings of the Bible on slavery. That field had been somewhat broken by our English predecessors. But in England the pro-slavery party had been soon shamed out of the attempt to drag the Bible into their service, and hence the discussion there had been short and somewhat superficial. The pro-slavery side of the question has been eagerly sustained by theological reviews and doctors of divinity without number, from the half-way and timid faltering of Wayland up to the unblushing and melancholy recklessness of Stuart. The argument on the other side has come wholly from the Abolitionists; for neither Dr. Hague nor Dr. Barnes can be said to have added any thing to the wide research, critical acumen, and comprehensive views of Theodore D. Weld, Beriah Green, J. G. Fee, and the old work of Duncan.

On the constitutional questions which have at various times arisen,—the citizenship of the colored man, the soundness of the "Prigg" decision, the constitutionality of the old Fugitive Slave Law, the true construction of the slave-surrender clause,—nothing has been added, either in the way of fact or argument, to the works of Jay, Weld, Alvan Stewart, E. G. Loring, S. E. Sewall, Richard Hildreth, W. I. Bowditch, the masterly essays of the *Emancipator* at New York and the *Liberator* at Boston, and the various addresses of the Massachusetts and American Societies for the last twenty years. The idea of the antislavery character of the Constitution,—the opiate with which Free Soil quiets its conscience for voting under a proslavery government,—I heard first suggested by Mr. Garrison in 1838. It was elaborately argued that year in all our antislavery gatherings, both here and in New York, and sustained with great ability by Alvan Stewart, and in part by T. D. Weld. The antislavery construction of the Constitution was ably argued in 1836, in the *Antislavery Magazine*, by Rev. Samuel J. May, one of the very first to seek the side of Mr. Garrison, and pledge to the slave his life and efforts,—a pledge which thirty years of devoted labors have redeemed. If it has either merit or truth, they are due to no legal learning recently added to our ranks, but to some of the old and well-known pioneers. This claim has since received the fullest investigation from Mr. Lysander Spooner, who has urged it with all his unrivalled ingenuity, laborious research, and close logic. He writes as a lawyer, and has no wish, I believe, to be ranked with any class of antislavery men.

The influence of slavery on our Government has received the profoundest philosophical investigation from the pen of Richard Hildreth, in his invaluable essay on "Despotism in America,"—a work which deserves a place by the side of the ablest political disquisitions of any age.

Even the vigorous mind of Rantoul, the ablest man, without doubt, of the Democratic party, and perhaps the ripest politician in New England, added little or nothing to the storehouse of antislavery argument. * * * His speeches on our question, too short and too few, are remarkable for their compact statement, iron logic, bold denunciation, and the wonderful light thrown back upon our history. Yet how little do they present which was not familiar for years in our antislavery meetings! Look, too, at the last great effort of the idol of so many thousands,—Mr. Senator Sumner,—the discussion of a great national question, of which it has been said that we must go back to Webster's reply to Hayne, and Fisher Ames on the Jay treaty, to find its equal in Congress,—praise which we might perhaps qualify, if any adequate report were left us of some of the noble orations of Adams. No one can be blind to the skilful use he has made of his materials, the consummate ability with which he has marshalled them, and the radiant glow which his genius has thrown over all. Yet, with the exception of his reference to the antislavery debate in Congress in 1817, there is hardly a train of thought or argument, and no single fact in the whole speech, which has not been familiar in our meetings and essays for the last ten years. * * *

The relations of the American Church to slavery, and the duties of private Christians, the whole casuistry of this portion of the question, so momentous among descendants of the Puritans,—have been discussed with great acuteness and rare common-sense by Messrs. Garrison, Goodell, Gerrit Smith, Pillsbury, and Foster. They have never attempted to judge the American Church by any standard except that which she has herself laid down,—never claimed that she should be perfect, but have contented themselves by demanding that she should be consistent. They have never judged her except out of her own mouth, and on facts asserted by her own presses and leaders. * * * In nothing have the Abolitionists shown more sagacity or more thorough knowledge of their countrymen than in the course they have pursued in relation to the Church. None but a New-Englander can appreciate the power which church organizations wield over all who share the blood of the Puritans. The influence of each sect over its own members is overwhelming, often shutting out, or controlling, all other influences. We have Popes here, all the more dangerous because no triple crown puts you on your guard. * * * In such a land, the Abolitionists early saw, that, for a moral question like theirs, only two paths lay open: to work through the Church; that failing, to join battle with it. Some tried long, like Luther, to be Protestants, and yet not come out of Catholicism; but their eyes were soon opened. Since then we have been convinced that, to come out from the Church, to hold her up as the bulwark of slavery, and to make her shortcomings the main burden of our appeals to the religious sentiment of the community, was our first duty and best policy. This course alienated many friends, and was a subject of frequent rebuke from such men as Dr. Channing. But nothing has ever more strengthened the cause, or won it more influence; and it has had the healthiest effect on the Church itself.

Unable to command a wide circulation for our books and journals, we have been obliged to bring ourselves into close contact with the people, and to rely mainly on public addresses.

These have been our most efficient instrumentality. For proof that these addresses have been full of pertinent facts, sound sense, and able arguments, we must necessarily point to results, and demand to be tried by our fruits. Within these last twenty years it has been very rare that any fact stated by your lecturers has been disproved, or any statement of theirs successfully impeached. And for evidence of the soundness, simplicity, and pertinency of their arguments we can only claim that our converts and co-laborers throughout the land have at least the reputation of being specially able " to give a reason for the faith that is in them."

I remember that when, in 1845, the present leaders of the Free Soil party, with Daniel Webster in their company, met to draw up the Anti-Texas Address of the Massachusetts Convention, they sent to Abolitionists for anti-slavery facts and history, for the remarkable testimonies of our Revolutionary great men which they wished to quote. When, many years ago, the Legislature of Massachusetts wished to send to Congress a resolution affirming the duty of immediate emancipation, the committee sent to William Lloyd Garrison to draw it up, and it stands now on our statute-book as he drafted it.

How vigilantly, how patiently, did we watch the Texas plot from its commencement! The politic South felt that its first move had been too bold, and thenceforward worked underground. For many a year men laughed at us for entertaining any apprehensions. It was impossible to rouse the North to its peril. David Lee Child was thought crazy because he would not believe there was no danger. His elaborate "Letters on Texan Annexation" are the ablest and most valuable contribution that has been made toward a history of the whole plot. Though we foresaw and proclaimed our conviction that annexation would be, in the end, a fatal step for the South, we did not feel at liberty to relax our opposition, well knowing the vast increase of strength it would give, at first, to the slave power. I remember being one of a committee which waited on Abbott Lawrence, a year or so only before annexation, to ask his countenance to some general movement, without distinction of party, against the Texas scheme. He smiled at our fears, begged us to have no apprehensions; stating that his correspondence with leading men at Washington enabled him to assure us annexation was impossible, and that the South itself was determined to defeat the project. A short time after, Senators and Representatives from Texas took their seats in Congress!

Many of these services to the slave were done before I joined his cause. In thus referring to them, do not suppose me merely seeking occasion of eulogy on my predecessors and present co-laborers. I recall these things only to rebut the contemptuous criticism which some about us make the excuse for their past neglect of the movement, and in answer to "Ion's" representation of our course as reckless fanaticism, childish impatience, utter lack of good sense, and of our meetings as scenes only of excitement, of reckless and indiscriminate denunciation. I assert that every social, moral, economical, religious, political, and historical aspect of the question has been ably and patiently examined. And all this has been done with an industry and ability which have left little for the professional skill, scholarly culture, and historical learning of the new laborers to accomplish. If the people are still in doubt, it is from the inherent difficulty of the subject, or a hatred of light, not from want of it. * * *

Sir, when a nation sets itself to do evil, and all its leading forces, wealth, party, and piety, join in the career, it is impossible but that those who offer a constant opposition should be hated and maligned, no matter how wise, cautious, and well planned their course may be. We are peculiar sufferers in this way. The community has come to hate its reproving Nathan so bitterly, that even those whom the relenting part of it are beginning to regard as standard-bearers of the antislavery host think it unwise to avow any connection or sympathy with him. I refer to some of the leaders of the political movement against slavery. They feel it to be their mission to marshal and use as effectively as possible the present convictions of the people. They cannot afford to encumber themselves with the odium which twenty years of angry agitation have engendered in great sects sore from unsparing rebuke, parties galled by constant defeat, and leading men provoked by unexpected exposure. They are willing to confess, privately, that our movement produced theirs, and that its continued existence is the very breath of their life. But, at the same time, they would fain walk on the road without being soiled by too close contact with the rough pioneers who threw it up. They are wise and honorable, and their silence is very expressive.

When I speak of their eminent position and acknowledged ability, another thought strikes me. Who converted these men and their distinguished associates? It is said we have shown neither sagacity in plans, nor candor in discussion, nor ability. Who, then, or what converted Burlingame and Wilson, Sumner and Adams, Palfrey and Mann, Chase and Hale, and Phillips and Giddings? Who taught the *Christian Register*, the *Daily Advertiser*, and that class of prints, that there were such things as a slave and a slave-holder in the land, and so gave them some more intelligent basis than their mere instincts to hate William Lloyd Garrison? What magic wand was it whose touch made the toadying servility of the land start up the real demon that it was, and at the same time gathered into the slave's service the professional ability, ripe culture, and personal integrity which grace the Free Soil ranks? We never argue! These men, then, were converted by simple denunciation! They were all converted by the "hot," "reckless," "ranting," "bigoted," "fanatic" Garrison, who never troubled himself about facts, nor stopped to argue with an opponent, but straightway knocked him down! My old and valued friend, Mr. Sumner, often boasts that he was a reader of the *Liberator* before I was. Do not criticise too much the agency by which such men were converted. That blade has a double edge. Our reckless course, our empty rant, our fanaticism, has made Abolitionists of some of the best and ablest men in the land. We are inclined to go on, and see if, even with such poor tools, we cannot make some more. Antislavery zeal and the roused conscience of the "godless come-outers" made the trembling South demand the Fugitive Slave Law, and the Fugitive Slave Law " provoked " Mrs. Stowe to the good work of " Uncle Tom." That is something! Let me say, in passing, that you will nowhere find an earlier or more generous appreciation, or more flowing eulogy, of these men and their labors, than in the columns of the *Liberator*. No one, however feeble, has ever peeped or muttered, in any quarter, that the vigilant eye of the Pioneer has not recognized him. He has stretched out the right hand of a most cordial welcome the moment any man's face was turned Zionward.

I do not mention these things to praise Mr. Garrison; I do not stand here for that purpose. You will not deny—if you do, I can prove it—

that the movement of the Abolitionists converted these men. Their constituents were converted by it. The assault upon the right of petition, upon the right to print and speak of slavery, the denial of the right of Congress over the District, the annexation of Texas, the Fugitive Slave Law, were measures which the antislavery movement provoked, and the discussion of which has made all the Abolitionists we have. The antislavery cause, then, converted these men; it gave them a constituency; it gave them an opportunity to speak, and it gave them a public to listen. The antislavery cause gave them their votes, got them their offices, furnished them their facts, gave them their audience. If you tell me they cherished all these principles in their own breasts before Mr. Garrison appeared, I can only say, if the antislavery movement did not give them their ideas, it surely gave the courage to utter them.

In such circumstances, is it not singular that the name of William Lloyd Garrison has never been pronounced on the floor of the United States Congress linked with any epithet but that of contempt! No one of those men who owe their ideas, their station, their audience, to him, have ever thought it worth their while to utter one word in grateful recognition of the power which called them into being. When obliged, by the course of their argument, to treat the question historically, they can go across the water to Clarkson and Wilberforce —yes, to a safe salt-water distance. As Daniel Webster, when he was talking to the farmers of Western New York, and wished to contrast slave labor and free labor, did not dare to compare New York with Virginia—sister States, under the same government, planted by the same race, worshipping at the same altar, speaking the same language—identical in all respects, save that one in which he wished to seek the contrast; but no; he compared it with Cuba— the contrast was so close! Catholic—Protestant; Spanish—Saxon; despotism—municipal institutions; readers of Lope de Vega and of Shakespeare; mutterers of the Mass—children of the Bible! But Virginia is too near home! So is Garrison! One would have thought there was something in the human breast which would sometimes break through policy. These noble-hearted men whom I have named must surely have found quite irksome the constant practice of what Dr. Gardiner used to call "that despicable virtue, prudence." One would have thought, when they heard that name spoken with contempt, their ready eloquence would have leaped from its scabbard to avenge even a word that threatened him with insult. But it never came—never! I do not say I blame them. Perhaps they thought they should serve the cause better by drawing a broad black line between themselves and him. Perhaps they thought the Devil could be cheated: I do not. * * *

Caution is not always good policy in a cause like ours. It is said that, when Napoleon saw the day going against him, he used to throw away all the rules of war, and trust himself to the hot impetuosity of his soldiers. The masses are governed more by impulse than conviction; and even were it not so, the convictions of most men are on our side, and this will surely appear, if we can only pierce the crust of their prejudice or indifference. I observe that our Free Soil friends never stir their audience so deeply as when some individual leaps beyond the platform, and strikes upon the very heart of the people. Men listen to discussions of laws and tactics with ominous patience. It is when Mr. Sumner, in Faneuil Hall, avows his determination to disobey the Fugitive Slave Law, and cries out: "I was a man before I was a Commissioner,"—when Mr. Giddings says of the fall of slavery, quoting Adams: "Let it come; if it must come in *blood*, yet I say let it come!"—that their associates on the platform are sure they are wrecking the party,—while many a heart beneath beats its first pulse of anti-slavery life.

These are brave words. When I compare them with the general tone of Free Soil men in Congress, I distrust the atmosphere of Washington and of politics. These men move about, Sauls and Goliaths among us, taller by many a cubit. There they lose port and stature. Mr. Sumner's speech in the Senate unsays no part of his Faneuil Hall pledge. But, though discussing the same topic, no one would gather from any word or argument that the speaker ever took such ground as he did in Faneuil Hall. It is all through, the *law*, the *manner* of the surrender, not the surrender itself, of the slave, that he objects to. As my friend Mr. Pillsbury so forcibly says, so far as any thing in the speech shows, he puts the slave behind the jury trial, behind the *habeas corpus* act, and behind the new interpretation of the Constitution, and says to the slave claimant: "You must get

through all these before you reach him; but, if
you *can* get through all these, you may have
him!" It was no tone like this which made
the old Hall rock! Not if he got through
twelve jury trials, and forty *habeas corpus* acts,
and constitutions built high as yonder monument, would he permit so much as the shadow
of a little finger of the slave claimant to touch
the slave! At least so he was understood.
* * * Mr. Mann, in his speech of February
15, 1850, says: "*The States being separated*, I
would as soon return my own brother or sister
into bondage, as I would return a fugitive slave.
Before God, and Christ, and all Christian men,
they are my brothers and sisters." What a
condition! From the lips, too, of a champion
of the Higher Law! Whether the States be
separate or united, neither my brother nor
any other man's brother shall, with my consent,
go back to bondage! So speaks the *heart*
—Mr. Mann's version is that of the politician. * * *

This seems to me a very mistaken strain.
Whenever slavery is banished from our national jurisdiction, it will be a momentous gain,
a vast stride. But let us not mistake the half-
way house for the end of the journey. I need

not say that it matters not to Abolitionists under what special law slavery exists. Their battle lasts while it exists anywhere, and I doubt not Mr. Sumner and Mr. Giddings feel themselves enlisted for the whole war. I will even suppose, what neither of these gentlemen states, that their plan includes not only that slavery shall be abolished in the District and Territories, but that the slave basis of representation shall be struck from the Constitution, and the slave-surrender clause construed away. But even then does Mr. Giddings or Mr. Sumner really believe that slavery, existing in its full force in the States, "will cease to vex our national politics"? Can they point to any State where a powerful oligarchy, possessed of immense wealth, has ever existed without attempting to meddle in the government? Even now, does not manufacturing, banking, and commercial capital perpetually vex our politics? Why should not slave capital exert the same influence? Do they imagine that a hundred thousand men, possessed of two thousand millions of dollars, which they feel the spirit of the age is seeking to tear from their grasp, will not eagerly catch at all the support they can obtain by getting the control of the government? In a land where the dollar is almighty, " where the sin of not being rich is only atoned for by the effort to become so," do they doubt that such an oligarchy will generally succeed? Besides, banking and manufacturing stocks are not urged by despair to seek a controlling influence in politics. They know they are about equally safe, whichever party rules—that no party wishes to legislate their rights away. Slave property knows that its being allowed to exist depends on its having the virtual control of the government. Its constant presence in politics is dictated, therefore, by despair, as well as by the wish to secure fresh privileges. Money, however, is not the only strength of the slave power. That, indeed, were enough, in an age when capitalists are our feudal barons. But, though driven entirely from national shelter, the slave-holders would have the strength of old associations, and of peculiar laws in their own States, which gives those States wholly into their hands. A weaker prestige, fewer privileges, and less comparative wealth, have enabled the British aristocracy to rule England for two centuries, though the root of their strength was cut at Naseby. It takes ages for deeply-rooted institutions to die; and driving slavery into the States will hardly be our Naseby. * * *

And Mr. Sumner "knows no better aim, under the Constitution, than to bring back the government" to where it was in 1789! Has the voyage been so very honest and prosperous a one, in his opinion, that his only wish is to start again with the same ship, the same crew, and the same sailing orders? Grant all he claims as to the state of public opinion, the intentions of leading men, and the form of our institutions at that period; still, with all these checks on wicked men, and helps to good ones, here we are, in 1853, according to his own showing, ruled by slavery, tainted to the core with slavery, and binding the infamous Fugitive Slave Law like an honorable frontlet on our brows. The more accurate and truthful his glowing picture of the public virtue of 1789, the stronger my argument. If even all those great patriots, and all that enthusiasm for justice and liberty, did not avail to keep us safe in such a Union, what will? In such desperate circumstances, can his statesmanship devise no better aim than to try the same experiment over again, under precisely the same conditions? What new guaranties does he propose to prevent the voyage from being again turned into a piratical slave-trading cruise? None! Have sixty years taught us nothing? In 1660, the English thought, in recalling Charles II., that the memory of that scaffold which had once darkened the windows of Whitehall would be guaranty enough for his good behavior. But, spite of the spectre, Charles II. repeated Charles I., and James outdid him. Wiser by this experience, when the nation in 1689 got another chance, they trusted to no guaranties, but so arranged the very elements of their government that William III. could not repeat Charles I. Let us profit by the lesson. * * *

If all I have said to you is untrue, if I have exaggerated, explain to me this fact. In 1831, Mr. Garrison commenced a paper advocating the doctrine of immediate emancipation. He had against him the thirty thousand churches and all the clergy of the country,—its wealth, its commerce, its press. In 1831, what was the state of things? There was the most entire ignorance and apathy on the slave question. If men knew of the existence of slavery, it was only as a part of picturesque Virginia life. No one preached, no one talked, no one wrote about it. No whisper of it stirred the surface of the political sea. The Church heard of it occasionally, when some colonization agent asked funds to send the blacks to Africa. Old school-books tainted with some antislavery selections had passed out of use, and new ones were compiled to suit the times. Soon as any dissent from the prevailing faith appeared, every one set himself to crush it. The pulpits preached at it; the press denounced it; mobs tore down houses, threw presses into the fire and the stream, and shot the editors; religious conventions tried to smother it; parties arrayed themselves against it. Daniel Webster boasted in the Senate, that he had never introduced the subject of slavery to that body, and never would. Mr. Clay, in 1839, makes a speech for the Presidency, in which he says, that to discuss the subject of slavery is moral treason, and that no man has a right to introduce the subject into Congress. Mr. Benton, in 1844, laid down his platform, and he not only denies the right, but asserts that he never has and never will discuss the subject. Yet Mr. Clay, from 1839 down to his death, hardly made a remarkable speech of any kind, except on slavery. Mr. Webster, having indulged now and then in a little easy rhetoric, as at Niblo's and elsewhere, opens his mouth in 1840, generously contributing his aid to both sides, and stops talking about it only when death closes his lips. Mr. Benton's six or eight speeches in the United States Senate have all been on the subject of slavery in the Southwestern section of the country, and form the basis of whatever claim he has to the character of a statesman, and he owes his seat in the next Congress somewhat, perhaps, to antislavery pretensions! The Whig and Democratic parties pledged themselves just as emphatically against the antislavery discussion, —against agitation and free speech. These men said: "It sha'n't be talked about; it won't be talked about!" These are *your statesmen!*—men who understand the present that is, and mould the future! The man who understands his own time, and whose genius moulds the future to his views, he is a statesman, is he not? These men devoted themselves to banks, to the tariff, to internal improvements, to constitutional and financial questions. They said to slavery: "Back! no entrance here! We pledge ourselves against you." And then there came up a little printer-boy, who whipped them into the traces, and made them talk, like Hotspur's starling, nothing BUT slavery. He scattered all these gigantic shadows,—tariff, bank, constitutional questions, financial questions; and slavery, like the colossal head in Walpole's romance, came up and filled the whole political horizon! Yet you must remember he is not a statesman; he is a "fanatic." He has no discipline,—Mr. "Ion" says so; he does not understand the "discipline that is essential to victory"! This man did not understand his own time, he did not know what the future was to be,—he was not able to shape it—he had no "prudence,"—he had no "foresight"! Daniel Webster says, "I have never introduced this subject, and never will,"—and dies broken-hearted because he had not been able to talk enough about it! Benton says, "I will never speak of slavery,"—and lives to break with his party on this issue! Clay says it is "moral treason" to introduce the subject into Congress—and lives to see Congress turned into an antislavery debating society, to suit the purpose of one "too powerful individual." * * * Remember who it was that said in 1831: "I am in earnest—I will not equivocate—I will not excuse—I will not retreat a single inch—*and I will be heard!*" That speaker has lived twenty-two years, and the complaint of twenty-three millions of people is, "Shall we never hear of any thing but slavery?" * * * Well, it is all HIS fault [pointing to Mr. Garrison]. * * * It seems to me that such men may point to the present aspect of the nation, to their originally avowed purpose, to the pledges and efforts of all your great men against them, and then let you determine to which side the credit of sagacity and statesmanship belongs. * * *

It may sound strange to some, this claim for Mr. Garrison of a profound statesmanship. Men have heard him styled a mere fanatic so long that they are incompetent to judge him fairly. "The phrases men are accustomed" says Goethe, "to repeat incessantly end by becoming convictions, and ossify the organs of intelligence." I cannot accept you, therefore, as my jury. I appeal from Festus to Cæsar, from the prejudice of our streets to the common-sense of the world, and to your children.

Every thoughtful and unprejudiced mind must see that such an evil as slavery will yield only to the most radical treatment. If you consider the work we have to do, you will not think us needlessly aggressive, or that we dig down unnecessarily deep in laying the foundations of our enterprise. A money power of two thousand millions of dollars, as the prices of slaves now range, held by a small body of able and desperate men; that body raised into a political aristocracy by special constitutional provisions; cotton, the product of slave labor, forming the basis of our whole foreign commerce, and the commercial class thus subsidized; the press bought up, the pulpit reduced to vassalage, the heart of the common people chilled by a bitter prejudice against the black race; our leading men bribed, by ambition, either to silence or open hostility; — in such a land, on what shall an Abolitionist rely? On a few cold prayers, mere lip-service, and never from the heart? On a church resolution, hidden often in its records, and meant only as a decent cover for servility in daily practice? On political parties, with their superficial influence at best, and seeking ordinarily only to use existing prejudices to the best advantage? Slavery has deeper root here than any aristocratic institution has in Europe; and politics is but the common pulse-beat, of which revolution is the fever-spasm. Yet we have seen European aristocracy survive storms which seemed to reach down to the primal strata of European life. Shall we, then, trust to mere politics, where even revolution has failed? How shall the stream rise above its fountain? Where shall our church organizations or parties get strength to attack their great parent and moulder, the slave power? Shall the thing formed say to him that formed it, Why hast thou made me thus? The old jest of one who tried to lift himself in his own basket, is but a tame picture of the man who imagines that, by working solely through existing sects and parties, he can destroy slavery. Mechanics say nothing but an earthquake strong enough to move all Egypt can bring down the pyramids.

Experience has confirmed these views. The Abolitionists who have acted on them have a "short method" with all unbelievers. They have but to point to their own success, in contrast with every other man's failure. To waken the nation to its real state, and chain it to the consideration of this one duty, is half the work. So much we have done. Slavery has been made the question of this generation. To startle the South to madness, so that every step she takes, in her blindness, is one step more toward ruin, is much. This we have done. Witness Texas and the Fugitive Slave Law. To have elaborated for the nation the only plan of redemption, pointed out the only exodus from this "sea of troubles," is much. This we claim to have done in our motto of IMMEDIATE, UNCONDITIONAL EMANCIPATION ON THE SOIL. The closer any statesmanlike mind looks into the question, the more favor our plan finds with it. The Christian asks fairly of the infidel, "If this religion be not from God, how do you explain its triumph, and the history of the first three centuries?" Our question is similar. If our agitation has not been wisely planned and conducted, explain for us the history of the last twenty years! Experience is a safe light to walk by, and he is not a rash man who expects success in future from the same means which have secured it in times past.

SALMON PORTLAND CHASE,

OF OHIO.

(BORN 1808, DIED 1873.)

ON THE KANSAS-NEBRASKA BILL; SENATE, FEBRUARY 3, 1854.

THE bill for the organization of the Territories of Nebraska and Kansas being under consideration—

Mr. CHASE submitted the following amendment:

Strike out from section 14 the words " was superseded by the principles of the legislation of 1850, commonly called the compromise measures, and "; so that the clause will read:

"That the Constitution, and all laws of the United States which are not locally inapplicable, shall have the same force and effect within the said Territory of Nebraska as elsewhere within the United States, except the eighth section of the act preparatory to the admission of Missouri into the Union, approved March 6, 1820, which is hereby declared inoperative."

Mr. CHASE said:

Mr. President, I had occasion, a few days ago to expose the utter groundlessness of the personal charges made by the Senator from Illinois (Mr. Douglas) against myself and the other signers of the Independent Democratic Appeal. I now move to strike from this bill a statement which I will to-day demonstrate to be without any foundation in fact or history. I intend afterward to move to strike out the whole clause annulling the Missouri prohibition.

I enter into this debate, Mr. President, in no spirit of personal unkindness. The issue is too grave and too momentous for the indulgence of such feelings. I see the great question before me, and that question only.

Sir, these crowded galleries, these thronged lobbies, this full attendance of the Senate, prove the deep, transcendent interest of the theme.

A few days only have elapsed since the Congress of the United States assembled in this Capitol. Then no agitation seemed to disturb the political elements. Two of the great political parties of the country, in their national conventions, had announced that slavery agitation was at an end, and that henceforth that subject was not to be discussed in Congress or out of Congress. The President, in his annual message, had referred to this state of opinion, and had declared his fixed purpose to maintain, as far as any responsibility attached to him, the quiet of the country. Let me read a brief extract from that message :

" It is no part of my purpose to give prominence to any subject which may properly be regarded as set at rest by the deliberate judgment of the people. But while the present is bright with promise, and the future full of demand and inducement for the exercise of active intelligence, the past can never be without useful lessons of admonition and instruction. If its dangers serve not as beacons, they will evidently fail to fulfil the object of a wise design. When the grave shall have closed over all those who are now endeavoring to meet the obligations of duty, the year 1850 will be recurred to as a period filled with anxious apprehension. A successful war had just terminated. Peace brought with it a vast augmentation of territory. Disturbing questions arose, bearing upon the domestic institutions of one portion of the Confederacy, and involving the constitutional rights of the States. But, notwitstanding differences of opinion and sentiment, which then existed in relation to details and specific provisions, the acquiescence of distinguished citizens, whose devotion to the Union can never be doubted, had given renewed vigor to our institutions, and restored a sense of repose and security to the public mind throughout the Confederacy. That this repose is to suffer no shock during my official term, if I have power to avert it, those who placed me here may be assured."

The agreement of the two old political parties, thus referred to by the Chief Magistrate of the country, was complete, and a large majority of the American people seemed to acquiesce in the legislation of which he spoke.

A few of us, indeed, doubted the accuracy of these statements, and the permanency of this repose. We never believed that the acts of 1850 would prove to be a permanent adjustment of the slavery question. We believed no permanent adjustment of that question possible except by a return to that original policy of the fathers of the Republic, by which slavery was restricted within State limits, and freedom, without exception or limitation, was intended to be secured to every person outside of State limits and under the exclusive jurisdiction of the General Government.

But, sir, we only represented a small, though vigorous and growing, party in the country. Our number was small in Congress. By some we were regarded as visionaries—by some as factionists; while almost all agreed in pronouncing us mistaken.

And so, sir, the country was at peace. As the eye swept the entire circumference of the horizon and upward to mid-heaven not a cloud appeared; to common observation there was no mist or stain upon the clearness of the sky.

But suddenly all is changed. Rattling thunder breaks from the cloudless firmament. The storm bursts forth in fury. Warring winds rush into conflict.

> "Eurus, Notusque ruunt, creberque procellis Africus."

Yes, sir, "*creber procellis Africus*"—the South wind thick with storm. And now we find ourselves in the midst of an agitation, the end and issue of which no man can foresee.

Now, sir, who is responsible for this renewal of strife and controversy? Not we, for we have introduced no question of territorial slavery into Congress—not we who are denounced as agitators and factionists. No, sir:

the quietists and the finalists have become agitators; they who told us that all agitation was quieted, and that the resolutions of the political conventions put a final period to the discussion of slavery.

This will not escape the observation of the country. It is *Slavery* that renews the strife. It is Slavery that again wants room. It is Slavery, with its insatiate demands for more slave territory and more slave States.

And what does Slavery ask for now? Why, sir, it demands that a time-honored and sacred compact shall be rescinded—a compact which has endured through a whole generation—a compact which has been universally regarded as inviolable, North and South—a compact, the constitutionality of which few have doubted, and by which all have consented to abide.

It will not answer to violate such a compact without a pretext. Some plausible ground must be discovered or invented for such an act; and such a ground is supposed to be found in the doctrine which was advanced the other day by the Senator from Illinois, that the compromise acts of 1850 "superseded" the prohibition of slavery north of 36° 30', in the act preparatory for the admission of Missouri. Ay, sir, "superseded" is the phrase—"superseded by the principles of the legislation of 1850, commonly called the compromise measures."

It is against this statement, untrue in fact, and without foundation in history, that the amendment which I have proposed is directed.

Sir, this is a novel idea. At the time when these measures were before Congress in 1850, when the questions involved in them were discussed from day to day, from week to week, and from month to month, in this Senate chamber, who ever heard that the Missouri prohibition was to be superseded? What man, at what time, in what speech, ever suggested the idea that the acts of that year were to affect the Missouri compromise? The Senator from Illinois the other day invoked the authority of Henry Clay—that departed statesman, in respect to whom, whatever may be the differences of political opinion, none question that, among the great men of this country, he stood proudly eminent. Did he, in the report made by him as the chairman of the Committee of Thirteen, or in any speech in support of the compromise acts, or in any conversation in the committee, or out of the committee, ever even hint at this doctrine of supersedure? Did any supporter or any opponent of the compromise acts ever vindicate or condemn them on the ground that the Missouri prohibition would be affected by them? Well, sir, the compromise acts were passed. They were denounced North, and they were denounced South. Did any defender of them at the South ever justify his support of them upon the ground that the South had obtained through them the repeal of the Missouri prohibition? Did any objector to them at the North ever even suggest as a ground of condemnation that that prohibition was swept away by them? No, sir! No man, North or South, during the whole of the discussion of those acts here, or in that other discussion which followed their enactment throughout the country, ever intimated any such opinion.

Now, sir, let us come to the last session of Congress. A Nebraska bill passed the House and came to the Senate, and was reported from the Committee on Territories by the Senator from Illinois, as its chairman. Was there any provision in it which even squinted toward this notion of repeal by supersedure? Why, sir, Southern gentlemen opposed it on the very ground that it left the Territory under the operation of the Missouri prohibition. The Senator from Illinois made a speech in defence of it. Did he invoke Southern support upon the ground that it superseded the Missouri prohibition? Not at all. Was it opposed or vindicated by anybody on any such ground? Every Senator knows the contrary. The Senator from Missouri (Mr. Atchison), now the President of this body, made a speech upon the bill, in which he distinctly declared that the Missouri prohibition was not repealed, and could not be repealed.

I will send this speech to the Secretary, and ask him to read the paragraphs marked.

The Secretary read as follows:

"I will now state to the Senate the views which induced me to oppose this proposition in the early part of this session.

"I had two objections to it. One was that the Indian title in that Territory had not been extinguished, or, at least, a very small portion of it had been. Another was the Missouri compromise, or, as it is commonly called, the slavery restriction. It was my opinion at that time—and I am not now very clear on that subject—that the law of Congress, when the State of Missouri was admitted into the Union, excluding slavery from the Territory of Louisiana north of 36° 30', would be enforced in that Territory unless it was specially rescinded, and whether that law was in accordance, with the Constitution of the United States or not, it would do its work, and that work would be to preclude slave-holders from going into that Territory. But when I came to look into that question, I found that there was no prospect, no hope, of a repeal of the Missouri compromise excluding slavery from that Territory. Now, sir, I am free to admit, that at this moment, at this hour, and for all time to come, I should oppose the organization or the settlement of that Territory unless my constituents, and the constituents of the whole South—of the slave States of the Union,—could go into it upon the same footing, with equal rights and equal privileges, carrying that species of property with them as other people of this Union. Yes, sir, I acknowledge that that would have governed me, but I have no hope that the restriction will ever be repealed.

"I have always been of opinion that the first great error committed in the political history of this country was the ordinance of 1787, rendering the Northwest Territory free territory. The next great error was the Missouri compromise. But they are both irremediable. There is no remedy for them. We must submit to them. I am prepared to do it. It is evident that the Missouri compromise cannot be repealed. So far as that question is concerned, we might as well agree to the admission of this Territory now as next year, or five or ten years hence."—*Congressional Globe*, Second Session, 32d Cong., vol. xxvi., page 1113.

That, sir, is the speech of the Senator from Missouri (Mr. Atchison), whose authority, I think, must go for something upon this question. What does he say? "When I came to look into that question"—of the possible repeal of the Missouri prohibition—that was the question he was looking into—"I found that there was no prospect, no hope, of a repeal of the Missouri compromise excluding slavery from that Territory." And yet, sir, at that very moment, according to this new doctrine of the Senator from Illinois, it had been repealed three years!

Well, the Senator from Missouri said further, that if he thought it possible to oppose this restriction successfully, he never would consent to the organization of the territory until it was rescinded. But, said he, "I acknowledge that I have no hope that the restriction will ever be repealed." Then he made some complaint, as other Southern gentlemen have frequently done, of the ordinance of 1787, and the Missouri prohibition; but went on to say: "They are both irremediable; there is no remedy for them; we must submit to them; I am prepared to do it; it is evident that the Missouri compromise cannot be repealed."

Now, sir, when was this said? It was on the morning of the 4th of March, just before the close of the last session, when that Nebraska bill, reported by the Senator from Illinois, which proposed no repeal, and suggested no supersedure, was under discussion. I think, sir, that all this shows pretty clearly that up to the very close of the last session of Congress nobody had ever thought of a repeal by supersedure. Then what took place at the commencement of the present session? The Senator from Iowa, early in December, introduced a bill for the organization of the Territory of Nebraska. I believe it was the same bill which was under discussion here at the last session, line for line, word for word. If I am wrong, the Senator will correct me.

Did the Senator from Iowa, then, entertain the idea that the Missouri prohibition had been superseded? No, sir, neither he nor any other man here, so far as could be judged from any discussion, or statement, or remark, had received this notion.

Well, on the 4th day of January, the Committee on Territories, through their chairman, the

Senator from Illinois, made a report on the territorial organization of Nebraska ; and that report was accompanied by a bill. Now, sir, on that 4th day of January, just thirty days ago, did the Committee on Territories entertain the opinion that the compromise acts of 1850 superseded the Missouri prohibition ? If they did, they were very careful to keep it to themselves. We will judge the committee by their own report. What do they say in that? In the first place they describe the character of the controversy, in respect to the Territories acquired from Mexico. They say that some believed that a Mexican law prohibiting slavery was in force there, while others claimed that the Mexican law became inoperative at the moment of acquisition, and that slave-holders could take their slaves into the Territory and hold them there under the provisions of the Constitution. The Territorial Compromise acts, as the committee tell us, steered clear of these questions. They simply provided that the States organized out of these Territories might come in with or without slavery, as they should elect, but did not affect the question whether slaves could or could not be introduced before the organization of State governments. That question was left entirely to judicial decision.

Well, sir, what did the committee propose to do with the Nebraska Territory? In respect to that, as in respect to the Mexican Territory, differences of opinion exist in relation to the introduction of slaves. There are Southern gentlemen who contend that notwithstanding the Missouri prohibition, they can take their slaves into the territory covered by it, and hold them there by virtue of the Constitution. On the other hand the great majority of the American people, North and South, believe the Missouri prohibition to be constitutional and effectual. Now, what did the committee propose? Did they propose to repeal the prohibition? Did they suggest that it had been superseded? Did they advance any idea of that kind? No, sir. This is their language:

"Under this section, as in the case of the Mexican law in New Mexico and Utah, it is a disputed point whether slavery is prohibited in the Nebraska country by valid enactment. The decision of this question involves the constitutional power of Congress to pass laws prescribing and regulating the domestic institutions of the various Territories of the Union. In the opinion of those eminent statesmen who hold that Congress is invested with no rightful authority to legislate upon the subject of slavery in the Territories, the eighth section of the act preparatory to the admission of Missouri is null and void, while the prevailing sentiment in a large portion of the Union sustains the doctrine that the Constitution of the United States secures to every citizen an inalienable right to move into any of the Territories with his property, of whatever kind and description, and to hold and enjoy the same under the sanction of law. Your committee do not feel themselves called upon to enter into the discussion of these controverted questions. They involve the same grave issues which produced the agitation, the sectional strife, and the fearful struggle of 1850."

This language will bear repetition:

"Your committee do not feel themselves called upon to enter into the discussion of these controverted questions. They involve the same grave issues which produced the agitation, the sectional strife, and the fearful struggle of 1850."

And they go on to say:

"Congress deemed it wise and prudent to refrain from deciding the matters in controversy then, either by affirming or repealing the Mexican laws, or by an act declaratory of the true intent of the Constitution and the extent of the protection afforded by it to slave property in the Territories; so your committee are not prepared now to recommend a departure from the course pursued on that memorable occasion, either by affirming or repealing the eighth section of the Missouri act, or by any act declaratory of the meaning of the Constitution in respect to the legal points in dispute."

Mr. President, here are very remarkable facts. The Committee on Territories declared that it was not wise, that it was not prudent, that it was not right, to renew the old controversy, and to arouse agitation. They declared that they would abstain from any recommendation of a repeal of the prohibition, or of any provision declaratory of the construction of the Constitution in respect to the legal points in dispute.

Mr. President, I am not one of those who suppose that the question between Mexican law and the slave-holding claims was avoided in the Utah and New Mexico Act; nor do I think that the introduction into the Nebraska bill of the provisions of those acts in respect to slavery would leave the question between the Missouri prohibition and the same slave-holding claims entirely unaffected. I am of a very different opinion. But I am dealing now with the report of the Senator from Illinois, as chairman of the committee, and I show, beyond all controversy, that that report gave no countenance whatever to the doctrine of repeal by supersedure.

Well, sir, the bill reported by the committee was printed in the *Washington Sentinel* on Saturday, January 7th. It contained twenty sections; no more, no less. It contained no provisions in respect to slavery, except those in the Utah and New Mexico bills. It left those provisions to speak for themselves. This was in harmony with the report of the committee. On the 10th of January—on Tuesday—the act appeared again in the *Sentinel;* but it had grown longer during the interval. It appeared now with twenty-one sections. There was a statement in the paper that the twenty-first section had been omitted by a clerical error.

But, sir, it is a singular fact that this twenty-first section is entirely out of harmony with the committee's report. It undertakes to determine the effect of the provision in the Utah and New Mexico bills. It declares, among other things, that all questions pertaining to slavery in the Territories, and in the new States to be formed therefrom, are to be left to the decision of the people residing therein, through their appropriate representatives. This provision, in effect, repealed the Missouri prohibition, which the committee, in their report, declared ought not to be done. Is it possible, sir, that this was a mere clerical error? May it not be that this twenty-first section was the fruit of some *Sunday work*, between Saturday the 7th, and Tuesday the 10th?

But, sir, the addition of this section, it seems, did not help the bill. It did not, I suppose, meet the approbation of Southern gentlemen, who contended that they have a right to take their slaves into the Territories, notwithstanding any prohibition, either by Congress or by a Territorial Legislature. I dare say it was found that the votes of these gentlemen could not be had for the bill with that clause in it. It was not enough that the committee had abandoned their report, and added this twenty-first section, in direct contravention of its reasonings and principles. The twenty-first section itself must be abandoned, and the repeal of the Missouri prohibition placed in a shape which would not deny the slave-holding claim.

The Senator from Kentucky (Mr. Dixon), on the 16th of January, submitted an amendment which came square up to repeal, and to the claim. That amendment, probably, produced some fluttering and some consultation. It met the views of Southern Senators, and probably determined the shape which the bill has finally assumed. Of the various mutations which it has undergone, I can hardly be mistaken in attributing the last to the amendment of the Senator from Kentucky. That there is no effect without a cause, is among our earliest lessons in physical philosophy, and I know of no causes which will account for the remarkable changes which the bill underwent after the 16th of January, other than that amendment, and the determination of Southern Senators to support it, and to vote against any provision recognizing the right of any Territorial Legislature to prohibit the introduction of slavery.

It was just seven days, Mr. President, after the Senator from Kentucky had offered his amendment, that a fresh amendment was reported from the Committee on Territories, in the shape of a new bill, enlarged to forty sections. This new bill cuts off from the proposed Territory half a degree of latitude on the south, and divides the residue into two Territories—the southern Territory of Kansas, and the northern Territory of Nebraska. It applies to each all the provisions of the Utah and New Mexico bills; it rejects entirely the twenty-first clerical-error section, and abrogates the Missouri prohibition by the very singular provision, which I will read:

"The Constitution and all laws of the United States which are not locally inapplicable shall have the same force and effect within the said Territory of Nebraska as elsewhere within the United States, except the eighth section of the act preparatory to the admission of Missouri into the Union, approved March 6, 1820, which was superseded by the principles of the legislation of 1850, commonly called the compromise measures, and is therefore declared inoperative."

Doubtless, Mr. President, this provision operates as a repeal of the prohibition. The Senator from Kentucky was right when he said it was in effect the equivalent of his amendment. Those who are willing to break up and destroy the old compact of 1820 can vote for this bill with full assurance that such will be its effect. But I appeal to them not to vote for this supersedure clause. I ask them not to incorporate into the legislation of the country a declaration which every one knows to be wholly untrue.

I have said that this doctrine of supersedure is new. I have now proved that it is a plant of but ten days' growth. It was never seen or heard of until the 23d day of January, 1854. It was upon that day that this tree of Upas was planted; we already see its poison fruits. * * *

The truth is, that the compromise acts of 1850 were not intended to introduce any principles of territorial organization applicable to any other Territory except that covered by them. The professed object of the friends of the compromise acts was to compose the whole slavery agitation. There were various matters of complaint. The non-surrender of fugitives from service was one. The existence of slavery and the slave-trade here in this District and elsewhere, under the exclusive jurisdiction of Congress, was another. The apprehended introduction of slavery into the Territories furnished other grounds of controversy. The slave States complained of the free States, and the free States complained of the slave States. It was supposed by some that this whole agitation might be stayed, and finally put at rest by skilfully adjusted legislation. So, sir, we had the omnibus bill, and its appendages the fugitive-slave bill and the District slave-trade suppression bill. To please the North—to please the free States—California was to be admitted, and the slave depots here in the District were to be broken up. To please the slave States, a stringent fugitive-slave act was to be passed, and slavery was to have a chance to get into the new Territories. The support of the Senators and Representatives from Texas was to be gained by a liberal adjustment of boundary, and by the assumption of a large portion of their State debt. The general result contemplated was a complete and final adjustment of all questions relating to slavery. The acts passed. A number of the friends of the acts signed a compact pledging themselves to support no man for any office who would in any way renew the agitation. The country was required to acquiesce in the settlement as an absolute finality. No man concerned in carrying those measures through Congress, and least of all the distinguished man whose efforts mainly contributed to their success, ever imagined that in the Territorial acts, which formed a part of the series, they were planting the germs of a new agitation. Indeed, I have proved that one of these acts contained an express stipulation which precludes the revival of the agitation in the form in which it is now thrust upon the country, without manifest disregard of the provisions of those acts themselves.

I have thus proved beyond controversy that the averment of the bill, which my amendment proposes to strike out, is untrue. Senators, will you unite in a statement which you know to be contradicted by the history of the country? Will you incorporate into a public statute an affirmation which is contradicted by every event which attended or followed the adoption of the compromise acts? Will you here, acting under your high responsibility as Senators of the States, assert as a fact, by a solemn vote, that which the personal recollection of every Senator who was here during the discussion of those compromise acts disproves? I will not believe it until I see it. If you wish to break up the time-honored compact embodied in the Missouri compromise, transferred into the joint resolution for the annexation of Texas, preserved and affirmed by these compromise acts themselves, do it openly—do it boldly. Repeal the Missouri prohibition. Repeal it by a direct vote. Do not repeal it by indirection. Do not "declare" it "inoperative," "because superseded by the principles of the legislation of 1850."

Mr. President, three great eras have marked the history of this country in respect to slavery. The first may be characterized as the Era of ENFRANCHISEMENT. It commenced with the earliest struggles for national independence. The spirit which inspired it animated the hearts and prompted the efforts of Washington, of Jefferson, of Patrick Henry, of Wythe, of Adams, of Jay, of Hamilton, of Morris—in short, of all the great men of our early history. All these hoped for, all these labored for, all these believed in, the final deliverance of the country from the curse of slavery. That spirit burned in the Declaration of Independence, and inspired the provisions of the Constitution, and the Ordinance of 1787. Under its influence, when in full vigor, State after State provided for the emancipation of the slaves within their limits, prior to the adoption of the Constitution. Under its feebler influence at a later period, and during the administration of Mr. Jefferson, the importation of slaves was prohibited into Mississippi and Louisiana, in the faint hope that those Territories might finally become free States. Gradually that spirit ceased to influence our public councils, and lost its control over the American heart and the American policy. Another era succeeded, but by such imperceptible gradations that the lines which separate the two cannot be traced with absolute precision. The facts of the two eras meet and mingle as the currents of confluent streams mix so imperceptibly that the observer cannot fix the spot where the meeting waters blend.

This second era was the Era of CONSERVATISM. Its great maxim was to preserve the existing condition. Men said: Let things remain as they are; let slavery stand where it is; exclude it where it is not; refrain from disturbing the public quiet by agitation; adjust all difficulties that arise, not by the application of principles, but by compromises.

It was during this period that the Senator tells us that slavery was maintained in Illinois, both while a Territory and after it became a State, in despite of the provisions of the ordinance. It is true, sir, that the slaves held in the Illinois country, under the French law, were not regarded as absolutely emancipated by the provisions of the ordinance. But full effect was given to the ordinance in excluding the introduction of slaves, and thus the Territory was preserved from eventually becoming a slave State. The few slave-holders in the Territory of Indiana, which then included Illinois, succeeded in obtaining such an ascendency in its affairs, that repeated applications were made not merely by conventions of delegates, but by the Territorial Legislature itself, for a suspension of the clause in the ordinance prohibiting slavery. These applications were reported upon by John Randolph, of Virginia, in the House, and by Mr. Franklin in the Senate. Both the reports were against suspension. The grounds stated by Randolph are specially worthy of being considered now. They are thus stated in the report:

"That the committee deem it highly dangerous and inexpedient to impair a provision wisely calculated to promote the happiness and prosperity of the Northwestern country, and to give strength and security to that extensive frontier. In the salutary operation of this sagacious and benevolent restraint, it is believed that the inhabitants of Indiana will, at no very distant day, find ample remuneration for a temporary privation of labor and of emigration."

Sir, these reports, made in 1803 and 1807, and the action of Congress upon them, in conformity with their recommendation, saved Illinois, and perhaps Indiana, from becoming slave States. When the people of Illinois formed their State constitution, they incorporated into it a section providing that neither slavery nor involuntary servitude shall hereafter be introduced into this State. The constitution made provision for the continued service of the few persons who were originally held as slaves, and then bound to service under the Territorial laws, and for the freedom of their children, and thus secured the final extinction of slavery. The Senator thinks that this result is not attributable to the ordinance. I differ from him. But for the ordinance, I have no doubt slavery would have been introduced into Indiana, Illinois, and Ohio. It is something to the credit of the Era of Conservatism, uniting its influences with those of the expiring Era of Enfranchisement, that it maintained the ordinance of 1787 in the Northwest.

The Era of CONSERVATISM passed, also by imperceptible gradations, into the Era of SLAVERY PROPAGANDISM. Under the influences of this new spirit we opened the whole territory acquired from Mexico, except California, to the ingress of slavery. Every foot of it was covered by a Mexican prohibition; and yet, by the legislation of 1850, we consented to expose it to the introduction of slaves. Some, I believe, have actually been carried into Utah and New Mexico. They may be few, perhaps, but a few are enough to affect materially the probable character of their future governments. Under the evil influences of the same spirit, we are now called upon to reverse the original policy of the Republic; to support even a solemn compact of the conservative period, and open Nebraska to slavery.

Sir, I believe that we are upon the verge of another era. That era will be the Era of REACTION. The introduction of this question here, and its discussion, will greatly hasten its advent. We, who insist upon the denationalization of slavery, and upon the absolute divorce of the General Government from all connection with it, will stand with the men who favored the compromise acts, and who yet wish to adhere to them, in their letter and in their spirit, against the repeal of the Missouri prohibition. But you may pass it here. You may send it to the other House. It may become a law. But its effect will be to satisfy all thinking men that no compromises with slavery will endure, except so long as they serve the interests of slavery; and that there is no safe and honorable ground for non-slaveholders to stand upon, except that of restricting slavery within State limits, and excluding it absolutely from the whole sphere of Federal jurisdiction. The old questions between political parties are at rest. No great question so thoroughly possesses the public mind as this of slavery. This discussion will hasten the inevitable reorganization of parties upon the new issues which our circumstances suggest. It will light up a fire in the country which may, perhaps, consume those who kindle it. * * *

CHARLES SUMNER,

OF MASSACHUSETTS.

(BORN 1811, DIED 1874.)

ON THE KANSAS-NEBRASKA BILL; SENATE, MAY 25, 1854.

I NOW present the remonstrance of a large number of citizens of New York against the repeal of the Missouri compromise.

I also present the memorial of the Religious Society of Friends, in Michigan, against the passage of the Nebraska bill, or any other bill annulling the Missouri compromise act of 1820.

I also present the remonstrance of the clergy and laity of the Baptist denomination in Michigan and Indiana, against the wrong and bad faith contemplated in the Nebraska bill. But this is not all.

I hold in my hand, and now present to the Senate, one hundred and twenty-five separate remonstrances from clergymen of every Protestant denomination in Maine, New Hampshire, Vermont, Massachusetts, Rhode Island, Connecticut, constituting the six New England States. These remonstrances are identical in character with the larger one presented by my distinguished colleague (Mr. Everett),—whose term of service here ends in a few days, by voluntary resignation, and who is now detained at home by illness,—and were originally intended as a part of it, but did not arrive in season to be annexed to that interesting and weighty document. They are independent in form, though supplementary in their nature—helping to swell the protests of the pulpits of New England. * * *

These remonstrances have especial significance, when it is urged, as it has been often in this debate, that the proposition still pending proceeds from the North. Yes, sir, proceeds from the North; for that is its excuse and apology. The ostrich is said to hide its head in the sand, and then vainly imagine its coward body beyond the reach of its pursuers. In similar spirit, honorable Senators seem to shelter themselves behind certain Northern votes, and then vainly imagine that they are protected from the judgment of the country. The pulpits of New England, representing to an unprecedented extent the popular voice there, now proclaim that these six States protest, with all the fervor of religious conviction, against this measure. To this extent, at least, I confidently declare it does not come from the North.

From these expressions, and other tokens which daily greet us, it is evident that at least the religious sentiment of the country is touched, and, under this sentiment, I rejoice to believe that the whole North will be quickened with the true life of freedom. Sir Philip Sidney, speaking to Queen Elizabeth of the spirit which animated every man, woman, and child in the Netherlands against the Spanish power, exclaimed : " It is the spirit of the Lord, and is invincible." A similar spirit is now animating the free States against the slave power, breathing everywhere its precious inspiration, and forbidding repose under the attempted usurpation. The threat of disunion, so often sounded in our ears, will be disregarded by an aroused and indignant people. Ah, sir, Senators vainly expect peace. Not in this way can peace come. In passing this bill, you scatter, broadcast through the land, dragon's teeth, and though they may not, as in ancient fable, spring up armed men, yet will they fructify in civil strife and feud.

From the depths of my soul, as a loyal citizen and as a Senator, I plead, remonstrate, protest against the passage of this bill. I struggle against it as against death; but, as in death itself corruption puts on incorruption, and this mortal body puts on immortality, so from the sting of this hour I find assurance of that triumph by which freedom will be restored to her immortal birthright in the Republic.

Sir, the bill, which you are now about to pass is at once the worst and the best bill on which Congress ever acted.

It is the worst bill, inasmuch as it is a present victory of slavery. In a Christian land, and in an age of civilization, a time-honored statute of freedom is struck down, opening the way to all the countless woes and wrongs of human bondage. Among the crimes of history a new one is about to be recorded, which, in better days, will be read with universal shame. The tea tax and stamp act, which aroused the patriotic rage of our fathers, were virtues by the side of this enormity; nor would it be easy to imagine, at this day, any measure which more openly defied every sentiment of justice, humanity, and Christianity. Am I not right, then, in calling it the worst bill on which Congress ever acted?

But there is another side to which I gladly turn. Sir, it is the best bill on which Congress ever acted; for it prepares the way for that "All hail hereafter," when slavery must disappear. It annuls all past compromises with slavery, and makes all future compromises impossible. Thus it puts freedom and slavery face to face, and bids them grapple. Who can doubt the result? It opens wide the door of the future, when, at last, there will really be a North, and the slave power will be broken; when this wretched despotism will cease to dominate over our Government, no longer impressing itself upon all that it does, at home and abroad; when the National Government shall be divorced in every way from slavery, and, according to the true intention of our fathers, freedom shall be established by Congress everywhere, at least beyond the local limits of the States.

Slavery will then be driven from its usurped foothold here in the District of Columbia; in the national Territories, and elsewhere beneath the national flag; the fugitive-slave bill, as odious as it is unconstitutional, will become a dead letter; and the domestic slave-trade, so far as it can be reached, but especially on the high seas, will be blasted by Congressional prohibition. Everywhere within the sphere of Congress, the great *Northern Hammer* will descend to smite the wrong; and the irresistible cry will break forth, "No more slave States!"

Thus, sir, now standing at the very grave of freedom in Kansas and Nebraska, I find assurances of that happy resurrection, by which freedom will be secured hereafter, not only in these Territories, but everywhere under the National Government. More clearly than ever before, I now see "the beginning of the end" of slavery. Am I not right, then, in calling this measure the best bill on which Congress ever acted?

Sorrowfully I bend before the wrong you are about to perpetrate. Joyfully I welcome all the promises of the future.

STEPHEN ARNOLD DOUGLAS,
OF ILLINOIS.
(BORN 1813, DIED 1861.)

ON THE KANSAS-NEBRASKA BILL; SENATE, MARCH 3, 1854.

It has been urged in debate that there is no necessity for these Territorial organizations; and I have been called upon to point out any public and national considerations which require action at this time. Senators seem to forget that our immense and valuable possessions on the Pacific are separated from the States and organized Territories on this side of the Rocky Mountains by a vast wilderness, filled by hostile savages—that nearly a hundred thousand emigrants pass through this barbarous wilderness every year, on their way to California and Oregon—that these emigrants are American citizens, our own constituents, who are entitled to the protection of law and government, and that they are left to make their way, as best they may, without the protection or aid of law or government. The United States mails for New Mexico and Utah, and official communications between this Government and the authorities of those Territories, are required to be carried over these wild plains, and through the gorges of the mountains, where you have made no provisions for roads, bridges, or ferries to facilitate travel, or forts or other means of safety to protect life. As often as I have brought forward and urged the adoption of measures to remedy these evils, and afford security against the damages to which our people are constantly exposed, they have been promptly voted down as not being of sufficient importance to command the favorable consideration of Congress. Now, when I propose to organize the Territories, and allow the people to do for themselves what you have so often refused to do for them, I am told that there are not white inhabitants enough permanently settled in the country to require and sustain a government. True; there is not a very large population there, for the very reason that your Indian code and intercourse laws exclude the settlers, and forbid their remaining there to cultivate the soil. You refuse to throw the country open to settlers, and then object to the organization of the Territories, upon the ground that there is not a sufficient number of inhabitants.

I will now proceed to the consideration of the great principle involved in the bill, without omitting, however, to notice some of those extraneous matters which have been brought into this discussion with the view of producing another antislavery agitation. We have been told by nearly every Senator who has spoken in opposition to this bill, that at the time of its introduction the people were in a state of profound quiet and repose, that the antislavery agitation had entirely ceased, and that the whole country was acquiescing cheerfully and cordially in the compromise measures of 1850 as a final adjustment of this vexed question. Sir, it is truly refreshing to hear Senators, who contested every inch of ground in opposition to those measures, when they were under discussion, who predicted all manner of evils and calamities from their adoption, and who raised the cry of appeal, and even resistance, to their execution, after they had become the laws of the land—I say it is really refreshing to hear these same Senators now bear their united testimony to the wisdom of those measures, and to the patriotic motives which induced us to pass them in defiance of their threats and resistance, and to their beneficial effects in restoring peace, harmony, and fraternity to a distracted country. These are precious confessions from the lips of those who stand pledged never to assent to the propriety of those measures, and to make war upon them, so long as they shall remain upon the statute-book. I well understand that these confessions are now made, not with the view of yielding their assent to the propriety of carrying those enactments into faithful execution, but for the purpose of having a pretext for charging upon me, as the author of this bill, the responsibility of an agitation which they are striving to produce. They say that I, and not they, have revived the agitation. What have I done to render me obnoxious to this charge? They say that I wrote and introduced this Nebraska bill. That is true; but I was not a volunteer in the transaction. The Senate, by a unanimous vote, appointed me chairman of the Territorial Committee, and associated five intelligent and patriotic Senators with me, and thus made it our duty to take charge of all Territorial business. In like manner, and with the concurrence of these complaining Senators, the Senate referred to us a distinct proposition to organize this Nebraska Territory, and required us to report specifically upon the question. I repeat, then, we were not volunteers in this business. The duty was imposed upon us by the Senate. We were not unmindful of the delicacy and responsibility of the position. We were aware that, from 1820 to 1850, the abolition doctrine of Congressional interference with slavery in the Territories and new States had so far prevailed as to keep up an incessant slavery agitation in Congress, and throughout the country, whenever any new Territory was to be acquired or organized. We were also aware that, in 1850, the right of the people to decide this question for themselves, subject only to the Constitution, was submitted for the doctrine of Congressional intervention. This first question, therefore, which the committee were called upon to decide, and indeed the only question of any material importance in framing this bill, was this: Shall we adhere to and carry out the principle recognized by the compromise measures of 1850, or shall we go back to the old exploded doctrine of Congressional interference, as established in 1820, in a large portion of the country, and which it was the object of the Wilmot proviso to give a universal application, not only to all the territory which we then possessed, but all which we might hereafter acquire? There are no alternatives. We were compelled to frame the bill upon the one or the other of these two principles. The doctrine of 1820 or the doctrine of 1850 must prevail. In the discharge of the duty imposed upon us by the Senate, the committee could not hesitate upon this point, whether we consulted our own individual opinions and principles, or those which were known to be entertained and boldly avowed by a large majority of the Senate. The two great political parties of the country stood solemnly pledged before the world to adhere to the compromise measures of 1850, "in principle and substance." A large majority of the Senate—indeed, every member of the body, I believe, except the two avowed Abolitionists (Mr. Chase and Mr. Sumner)—profess to belong to one or the other of these parties, and hence were supposed to be under a high moral obligation to carry out "the principle and substance" of those measures in all new Territorial organizations. The report of the committee was in accordance with this obligation. I am arraigned, therefore, for having endeavored to represent the opinions and principles of the Senate truly—for having performed my duty in conformity with parliamentary law —for having been faithful to the trust imposed in me by the Senate. Let the vote this night determine whether I have thus faithfully represented your opinions. When a majority of the Senate shall have passed the bill—when the majority of the States shall have endorsed it through their representatives upon this floor— when a majority of the South and a majority of the North shall have sanctioned it—when a majority of the Whig party and a majority of the Democratic party shall have voted for it— when each of these propositions shall be demonstrated by the vote this night on the final passage of the bill, I shall be willing to submit the question to the country, whether, as the organ of the committee, I performed my duty in the report and bill which have called down upon my head so much denunciation and abuse.

Mr. President, the opponents of this measure have had much to say about the mutations and modifications which this bill has undergone since it was first introduced by myself, and about the alleged departure of the bill, in its present form, from the principle laid down in the original report of the committee as a rule of action in all future Territorial organizations. Fortunately there is no necessity, even if your patience would tolerate such a course of argument at this late hour of the night, for me to examine these speeches in detail, and reply to each charge separately. Each speaker seems to have followed faithfully in the footsteps of his leader in the path marked out by the Abolition confederates in their manifesto, which I took occasion to expose on a former occasion. You have seen them on their winding way, meandering the narrow and crooked path in Indian file, each treading close upon the heels of the other, and neither venturing to take a step to the right or left, or to occupy one inch of ground which did not bear the footprint of the Abolition champion. To answer one, therefore, is to answer the whole. The statement to which they seem to attach the most importance, and which they have repeated oftener, perhaps, than any other, is, that, pending the compromise measures of 1850, no man in or out of Congress ever dreamed of abrogating the Missouri compromise; that from that period down to the present session nobody supposed that its validity had been impaired, or any thing done which rendered it obligatory upon us to make it inoperative hereafter; that at the time of submitting the report and bill to the Senate, on the fourth of January last, neither I nor any member of the committee ever thought of such a thing; and that we could never be brought to the point of abrogating the eighth section of the Missouri act until after the Senator from Kentucky introduced his amendment to my bill.

Mr. President, before I proceed to expose the many misrepresentations contained in this complicated charge, I must call the attention of the Senate to the false issue which these gentlemen are endeavoring to impose upon the country, for the purpose of diverting public attention from the real issue contained in the bill. They wish to have the people believe that the abrogation of what they call the Missouri compromise was the main object and aim of the bill, and that the only question involved is, whether the prohibition of slavery north of 36° 30′ shall be repealed or not? That which is a mere incident they choose to consider the principal. They make war on the means by which we propose to accomplish an object, instead of openly resisting the object itself. The principle which we propose to carry into effect by the bill is this: That *Congress shall neither legislate slavery into any Territories or State, nor out of the same; but the people shall be left free to regulate their domestic concerns in their own way, subject only to the Constitution of the United States.*

In order to carry this principle into practical operation, it becomes necessary to remove whatever legal obstacles might be found in the way of its free exercise. It is only for the purpose of carrying out this great fundamental principle of self-government that the bill renders the eighth section of the Missouri act inoperative and void.

Now, let me ask, will these Senators who have arraigned me, or any one of them, have the assurance to rise in his place and declare that this great principle was never thought of or advocated as applicable to Territorial bills, in 1850; that from that session until the present, nobody ever thought of incorporating this principle in all new Territorial organizations; that the Committee on Territories did not recommend it in their report; and that it required the amendment of the Senator from Kentucky to bring us up to that point? Will any one of my accusers dare to make this issue, and let it be tried by the record? I will begin with the compromises of 1850, Any Senator who will take the trouble to examine our journals, will find that on the 25th of March of that year I reported from the Committee on Territories two bills including the following measures; the admission of California, a Territorial government for New Mexico, and the adjustment of the Texas boundary. These bills proposed to leave the people of Utah and New Mexico free to decide the slavery question for themselves, *in the precise language of the Nebraska bill now under discussion.* A few weeks afterward the committee of thirteen took those two bills and put a wafer between them, and reported them back to the Senate as one bill, with some slight amendments. One of these amendments was, that the Territorial Legislatures should not legislate upon the subject of African slavery. I objected to that provision upon the ground that it subverted the great principle of self-government upon which the bill had been originally framed by the Territorial Committee. On the first trial, the Senate refused to strike it out, but subsequently did so, after full debate, in order to establish that principle as the rule of action in Territorial organizations. But my accusers attempt to raise up a false issue, and thereby divert public attention from the real one, by the cry that the Missouri compromise is to be repealed or violated by the passage of this bill. Well, if the eighth section of the Missouri act, which attempted to fix the destinies of future generations in those Territories for all time to come, in utter disregard of the rights and wishes of the people when they should be received into the Union as States, be inconsistent with the great principles of self-government and the Constitution of the United States, it ought to be abrogated. The legislation of 1850 abrogated the Missouri compromise, so far as the country embraced within the limits of Utah and New Mexico was covered by the slavery restriction. It is true, that those acts did not in terms and by name repeal the act of 1820, as originally adopted, or as extended by the resolutions annexing Texas in 1845, any more than the report of the Committee on Territories proposed to repeal the same acts this session. But the acts of 1850 did authorize the people of those Territories to exercise "all rightful powers of legislation consistent with the Constitution," not excepting the question of slavery; and did provide that, when those Territories should be admitted into the Union, they should be received with or without slavery as the people thereof might determine at the date of their admission. These provisions were in direct conflict with a clause in the former enactment, declaring that slavery should be forever prohibited in any portion of said Territories, and hence rendered such clause inoperative and void to the extent of such conflict. This was an inevitable consequence, resulting from the provisions in those acts, which gave the people the right to decide the slavery question for themselves, in conformity with the Constitution. It was not necessary to go farther and declare that certain previous enactments, which were incompatible with the exercise of the powers conferred in the bills, are hereby repealed. The very act of granting those powers and rights has the legal effect of removing all obstructions to the exercise of them by the people, as prescribed in those Territorial bills. Following that example, the Committee on Territories did not consider it necessary to declare the eighth section of the

Missouri act repealed. We were content to organize Nebraska in the precise language of the Utah and New Mexican bills. Our object was to leave the people entirely free to form and regulate their domestic institutions and internal concerns in their own way, under the Constitution; and we deemed it wise to accomplish that object in the exact terms in which the same thing had been done in Utah and New Mexico by the acts of 1850. This was the principle upon which the committee voted; and our bill was supposed, and is now believed, to have been in accordance with it. When doubts were raised whether the bill did fully carry out the principle laid down in the report, amendments were made from time to time, in order to avoid all misconstruction, and make the true intent of the act more explicit. The last of these amendments was adopted yesterday, on the motion of the distinguished Senator from North Carolina (Mr. Badger), in regard to the revival of any laws or regulations which may have existed prior to 1820. That amendment was not intended to change the legal effect of the bill. Its object was to repel the slander which had been propagated by the enemies of the measure in the North—

that the Southern supporters of the bill desired to legislate slavery into these Territories. The South denies the right of Congress either to legislate slavery into any Territory or State, or out of any Territory or State. Non-intervention by Congress with slavery in the States or Territories is the doctrine of the bill, and all the amendments which have been agreed to have been made with the view of removing all doubt and cavil as to the true meaning and object of the measure * * *

Well, sir, what is this Missouri compromise, of which we have heard so much of late? It has been read so often that it is not necessary to occupy the time of the Senate in reading it again. It was an act of Congress, passed on the 6th of March, 1820, to authorize the people of Missouri to form a constitution and a State government, preparatory to the admission of such State into the Union. The first section provided that Missouri should be received into the Union "on an equal footing with the original States in all respects whatsoever." The last and eighth section provided that slavery should be "forever prohibited" in all the territory which had been acquired from France north of 36° 30′, and not included within the limits of the State of Missouri. There is nothing in the terms of the law that purports to be a compact, or indicates that it was any thing more than an ordinary act of legislation. To prove that it was more than it purports to be on its face, gentlemen must produce other evidence, and prove that there was such an understanding as to create a moral obligation in the nature of a compact. Have they shown it?

Now, if this was a compact, let us see how it was entered into. The bill originated in the House of Representatives, and passed that body without a Southern vote in its favor. It is proper to remark, however, that it did not at that time contain the eighth section, prohibiting slavery in the Territories; but in lieu of it, contained a provision prohibiting slavery in the proposed State of Missouri. In the Senate, the clause prohibiting slavery in the State was stricken out, and the eighth section added to the end of the bill, by the terms of which slavery was to be forever prohibited in the territory not embraced in the State of Missouri north of 36° 30′. The vote on adding this section stood in the Senate, 34 in the affirmative, and 10 in the negative. Of the

Northern Senators, 20 voted for it, and 2 against it. On the question of ordering the bill to a third reading as amended, which was the test vote on its passage, the vote stood 24 yeas and 20 nays. Of the Northern Senators, 4 only voted in the affirmative, and 18 in the negative. Thus it will be seen that if it was intended to be a compact, the North never agreed to it. The Northern Senators voted to insert the prohibition of slavery in the Territories; and then, in the proportion of more than four to one, voted against the passage of the bill. The North, therefore, never signed the compact, never consented to it, never agreed to be bound by it. This fact becomes very important in vindicating the character of the North for repudiating this alleged compromise a few months afterward. The act was approved and became a law on the 6th of March, 1820. In the summer of that year, the people of Missouri formed a constitution and State government preparatory to admission into the Union in conformity with the act. At the next session of Congress the Senate passed a joint resolution declaring Missouri to be one of the States of the Union, on an equal footing with the original States. This resolution was sent to the House of Representatives, where it was rejected by Northern votes, and thus Missouri was voted out of the Union, instead of being received into the Union under the act of the 6th of March, 1820, now known as the Missouri compromise. Now, sir, what becomes of our plighted faith, if the act of the 6th of March, 1820, was a solemn compact, as we are now told? They have all rung the changes upon it, that it was a sacred and irrevocable compact, binding in honor, in conscience, and morals, which could not be violated or repudiated without perfidy and dishonor! * * * Sir, if this was a compact, what must be thought of those who violated it almost immediately after it was formed? I say it is a calumny upon the North to say that it was a compact. I should feel a flush of shame upon my cheek, as a Northern man, if I were to say that it was a compact, and that the section of the country to which I belong received the consideration, and then repudiated the obligation in eleven months after it was entered into. I deny that it was a compact, in any sense of the term. But if it was, the record proves that faith was not observed —that the contract was never carried into effect —that after the North had procured the passage of the act prohibiting slavery in the Territories, with a majority in the House large enough to prevent its repeal, Missouri was refused admission into the Union as a slave-holding State, in conformity with the act of March 6, 1820. If the proposition be correct, as contended for by the opponents of this bill—that there was a solemn compact between the North and South that, in the consideration of the prohibition of slavery in the Territories, Missouri was to be admitted into the Union, in conformity with the act of 1820—that compact was repudiated by the North, and rescinded by the joint action of the two parties within twelve months from its date. Missouri was never admitted under the act of the 6th of March, 1820. She was refused admission under that act. She was voted out of the Union by Northern votes, notwithstanding the stipulation that she should be received; and, in consequence of these facts, a new compromise was rendered necessary, by the terms of which Missouri was to be admitted into the Union conditionally—admitted on a condition not embraced in the act of 1820, and, in addition, to a full compliance with all the provisions of said act. If, then, the act of 1820, by the eighth section of which slavery was prohibited in Missouri, was a compact, it is clear to the comprehension of every fair-minded man that the refusal of the North to admit Missouri, in compliance with its stipulations, and without further conditions, imposes upon us a high, moral obligation to remove the prohibition of slavery in the Territories, since it has been shown to have been procured upon a condition never performed.

Mr. President, I did not wish to refer to these things. I did not understand them fully in all their bearings at the time I made my first speech on this subject; and, so far as I was familiar with them, I made as little reference to them as was consistent with my duty; because it was a mortifying reflection to me, as a Northern man, that we had not been able, in consequence of the abolition excitement at the time, to avoid the appearance of bad faith in the observance of legislation, which has been denominated a compromise. There were a few men then, as there are now, who had the moral courage to perform their duty to the country and the Constitution, regardless of consequences personal to themselves. There were ten Northern men who dared to perform their duty by voting to admit Missouri into the

Union on an equal footing with the original States, and with no other restriction than that imposed by the Constitution. I am aware that they were abused and denounced as we are now—that they were branded as dough-faces—traitors to freedom, and to the section of country whence they came. * * *

I think I have shown that if the act of 1820, called the Missouri compromise, was a compact, it was violated and repudiated by a solemn vote of the House of Representatives in 1821, within eleven months after it was adopted. It was repudiated by the North by a majority vote, and that repudiation was so complete and successful as to compel Missouri to make a new compromise, and she was brought into the Union under the new compromise of 1821, and not under the act of 1820. This reminds me of another point made in nearly all the speeches against this bill, and, if I recollect right, was alluded to in the abolition manifesto; to which, I regret to say, I had occasion to refer so often. I refer to the significant hint that Mr. Clay was dead before any one dared to bring forward a proposition to undo the greatest work of his hands. The Senator from New York (Mr. Seward) has seized upon this insinuation and elaborated, perhaps, more fully than his compeers; and now the Abolition press, suddenly, and, as if by miraculous conversion, teems with eulogies upon Mr. Clay and his Missouri compromise of 1820.

Now, Mr. President, does not each of these Senators know that Mr. Clay was not the author of the act of 1820? Do they not know that he disclaimed it in 1850 in this body? Do they not know that the Missouri restriction did not originate in the House, of which he was a member? Do they not know that Mr. Clay never came into the Missouri controversy as a compromiser until after the compromise of 1820 was repudiated, and it became necessary to make another? I dislike to be compelled to repeat what I have conclusively proven, that the compromise which Mr. Clay effected was the act of 1821, under which Missouri came into the Union, and not the act of 1820. Mr. Clay made that compromise after you had repudiated the first one. How, then, dare you call upon the spirit of that great and gallant statesman to sanction your charge of bad faith against the South on this question? * * *

Now, Mr. President, as I have been doing justice to Mr. Clay on this question, perhaps I may as well do justice to another great man, who was associated with him in carrying through the great measures of 1850, which mortified the Senator from New York so much, because they defeated his purpose of carrying on the agitation. I allude to Mr. Webster. The authority of his great name has been quoted for the purpose of proving that he regarded the Missouri act as a compact, an irrepealable compact. Evidently the distinguished Senator from Massachusetts (Mr. Everett) supposed he was doing Mr. Webster entire justice when he quoted the passage which he read from Mr. Webster's speech of the 7th of March, 1850, when he said that he stood upon the position that every part of the American continent was fixed for freedom or for slavery by irrepealable law. The Senator says that by the expression "irrepealable law," Mr. Webster meant to include the compromise of 1820. Now, I will show that that was not Mr. Webster's meaning—that he was never guilty of the mistake of saying that the Missouri act of 1820 was an irrepealable law. Mr. Webster said in that speech that every foot of territory in the United States was fixed as to its character for freedom or slavery by an irrepealable law. He then inquired if it was not so in regard to Texas? He went on to prove that it was; because, he said, there was a compact in express terms between Texas and the United States. He said the parties were capable of contracting and that there was a valuable consideration; and hence, he contended, that in that case there was a contract binding in honor and morals and law; and that it was irrepealable without a breach of faith.

He went on to say:

"Now, as to California and New Mexico, I hold slavery to be excluded from these Territories by a law even superior to that which admits and sanctions it in Texas—I mean the law of nature—of physical geography—the law of the formation of the earth."

That was the irrepealable law which he said prohibited slavery in the Territories of Utah and New Mexico. He went on to speak of the prohibition of slavery in Oregon, and he said it was an "entirely useless and, in that connection, senseless proviso."

He went further, and said:

"That the whole territory of the States of the United States, or in the newly-acquired territory of the United States, has a fixed and settled character, now fixed and settled by law, which cannot be repealed in the case of Texas without a violation of public faith, and cannot be repealed by any human power in regard to California or New Mexico; that, *under one or other of these laws,* every foot of territory in the States or in the Territories has now received a fixed and decided character."

What irrepealable laws? "One or the other" of those which he had stated. One was the Texas compact; the other, the law of nature and physical geography; and he contended that one or the other fixed the character of the whole American continent for freedom or for slavery. He never alluded to the Missouri compromise, unless it was by the allusion to the Wilmot proviso in the Oregon bill, and therein said it was a useless and, in that connection, senseless thing. Why was it a useless and senseless thing? Because it was re-enacting the law of God; because slavery had already been prohibited by physical geography. Sir, that was the meaning of Mr. Webster's speech. * * *

Mr. President, I have occupied a good deal of time in exposing the cant of these gentlemen about the sanctity of the Missouri compromise, and the dishonor attached to the violation of plighted faith. I have exposed these matters in order to show that the object of these men is to withdraw from public attention the real principle involved in the bill. They well know that the abrogation of the Missouri compromise is the incident and not the principal of the bill. They well understand that the report of the committee and the bill propose to establish the principle in all Territorial organizations, that the question of slavery shall be referred to the people to regulate for themselves, and that such legislation should be had as was necessary to remove all legal obstructions to the free exercise of this right by the people. The eighth section of the Missouri act standing in the way of this great principle must be rendered inoperative and void, whether expressly repealed or not, in order to give the people the power of regulating their own domestic institutions in their own way, subject only to the Constitution.

Now, sir, if these gentlemen have entire confidence in the correctness of their own position, why do they not meet the issue boldly and fairly, and controvert the soundness of this great principle of popular sovereignty in obedience to the Constitution? They know full well that this was the principle upon which the colonies separated from the crown of Great Britain, the principle upon which the battles of the Revolution were fought, and the principle upon which our republican system was founded. They cannot be ignorant of the fact that the Revolution grew out of the assertion of the right on the part of the imperial Government to interfere with the internal affairs and domestic concerns of the colonies. * * *

The Declaration of Independence had its origin in the violation of that great fundamental principle which secured to the colonies the right to regulate their own domestic affairs in their own way; and the Revolution resulted in the triumph of that principle, and the recognition of the right asserted by it. Abolitionism proposes to destroy the right and extinguish the principle for which our forefathers waged a seven years' bloody war, and upon which our whole system of free government is founded. They not only deny the application of this principle to the Territories, but insist upon fastening the prohibition upon all the States to be formed out of those Territories. Therefore, the doctrine of the Abolitionists—the doctrine of the opponents of the Nebraska and Kansas bill, and the advocates of the Missouri restriction—demands Congressional interference with slavery not only in the Territories, but in all the new States to be formed therefrom. It is the same doctrine, when applied to the Territories and new States of this Union, which the British Government attempted to enforce by the sword upon the American colonies. It is this fundamental principle of self-government which constitutes the distinguishing feature of the Nebraska bill. The opponents of the principle are consistent in opposing the bill. I do not blame them for their opposition. I only ask them to meet the issue fairly and openly, by acknowledging that they are opposed to the principle which it is the object of the bill to carry into operation. It seems that there is no power on earth, no intellectual power, no mechanical power, that can bring them to a fair discussion of the true issue. If they hope to delude the people and escape detection for any considerable length of time under the catch-words "Missouri compromise" and "faith of compacts," they will find that the people of this country have more penetration and intelligence than they have given them credit for.

Mr. President, there is an important fact connected with this slavery regulation, which should never be lost sight of. It has always arisen from one and the same cause. Whenever that cause has been removed, the agitation has ceased; and whenever the cause has been renewed, the agitation has sprung into existence. That cause is, and ever has been, the attempt on the part of Congress to interfere with the question of slavery in the Territories and new States formed therefrom. Is it not wise then to confine our action within the sphere of our legitimate duties, and leave this vexed question to take care of itself in each State and Territory, according to the wishes of the people thereof, in conformity to the forms, and in subjection to the provisions, of the Constitution?

The opponents of the bill tell us that agitation is no part of their policy; that their great desire is peace and harmony; and they complain bitterly that I should have disturbed the repose of the country by the introduction of this measure! Let me ask these professed friends of peace, and avowed enemies of agitation, how the issue could have been avoided. They tell me that I should have let the question alone; that is, that I should have left Nebraska unorganized, the people unprotected, and the Indian barrier in existence, until the swelling tide of emigration should burst through, and accomplish by violence what it is the part of wisdom and statesmanship to direct and regulate by law. How long could you have postponed action with safety? How long could you maintain that Indian barrier, and restrain the onward march of civilization, Christianity, and free government by a barbarian wall? Do you suppose that you could keep that vast country a howling wilderness in all time to come, roamed over by hostile savages, cutting off all safe communication between our Atlantic and Pacific possessions? I tell you that the time for action has come, and cannot be postponed. It is a case in which the "let-alone" policy would precipitate a crisis which must inevitably result in violence, anarchy, and strife.

You cannot fix bounds to the onward march of this great and growing country. You cannot fetter the limbs of the young giant. He will burst all your chains. He will expand, and grow, and increase, and extend civilization, Christianity, and liberal principles. Then, sir, if you cannot check the growth of the country in that direction, is it not the part of wisdom to look the danger in the face, and provide for an event which you cannot avoid? I tell you, sir, you must provide for lines of continuous settlement from the Mississippi valley to the Pacific ocean. And in making this provision, you must decide upon what principles the Territories shall be organized; in other words, whether the people shall be allowed to regulate their domestic institutions in their own way, according to the provisions of this bill, or whether the opposite doctrine of Congressional interference is to prevail. Postpone it, if you will; but whenever you do act, this question must be met and decided.

The Missouri compromise was interference; the compromise of 1850 was non-interference, leaving the people to exercise their rights under the Constitution. The Committee on Territories were compelled to act on this subject. I, as their chairman, was bound to meet the question. I chose to take the responsibility regardless of consequences personal to myself. I should have done the same thing last year, if there had been time; but we know, considering the late period at which the bill then reached us from the House, that there was not sufficient time to consider the question fully, and to prepare a report upon the subject.

I was, therefore, persuaded by my friends to allow the bill to be reported to the Senate, in order that such action might be taken as should be deemed wise and proper. The bill was never taken up for action—the last night of the session having been exhausted in debate on a motion to take up the bill. This session, the measure was introduced by my friend from Iowa (Mr. Dodge), and referred to the Territorial Committee during the first week of the session. We have abundance of time to consider the subject; it is a matter of pressing necessity, and there was no excuse for not meeting it directly and fairly. We were compelled to take our position upon the doctrine either of intervention or non-intervention. We chose the latter for two reasons: first, because we believed that the principle was right; and, second, because it was the principle adopted in 1850, to which the two great political parties of the country were solemnly pledged.

There is another reason why I desire to see this principle recognized as a rule of action in all time to come. It will have the effect to destroy all sectional parties and sectional agitations. If, in the language of the report of the committee, you withdraw the slavery question from the halls of Congress and the political arena, and commit it to the arbitrament of those who are immediately interested in and alone responsible for its consequences, there is nothing left out of which sectional parties can be organized. It never was done, and never can be done on the bank, tariff, distribution, or any party issue which has existed, or may exist, after this slavery question is withdrawn from politics. On every other political question these have always supporters and opponents in every portion of the Union—in each State, county, village, and neighborhood—residing together in harmony and good fellowship, and combating each other's opinions and correcting each other's errors in a spirit of kindness and friendship. These differences of opinion between neighbors and friends, and the discussions that grow out of them, and the sympathy which each feels with the advocates of his own opinions in every portion of this widespread Republic, add an overwhelming and irresistible moral weight to the strength of the Confederacy. Affection for the Union can never be alienated or diminished by any other party issues than those which are joined upon sectional or geographical lines. When the people of the

North shall all be rallied under one banner, and the whole South marshalled under another banner, and each section excited to frenzy and madness by hostility to the institutions of the other, then the patriot may well tremble for the perpetuity of the Union. Withdraw the slavery question from the political arena, and remove it to the States and Territories, each to decide for itself, such a catastrophe can never happen. Then you will never be able to tell, by any Senator's vote for or against any measure, from what State or section of the Union he comes.

Why, then, can we not withdraw this vexed question from politics? Why can we not adopt the principle of this bill as a rule of action in all new Territorial organizations? Why can we not deprive these agitators of their vocation and render it impossible for Senators to come here upon bargains on the slavery question? I believe that the peace, the harmony, and perpetuity of the Union require us to go back to the doctrines of the Revolution, to the principles of the Constitution, to the principles of the Compromise of 1850, and leave the people, under the Constitution, to do as they may see proper in respect to their own internal affairs.

Mr. President, I have not brought this question forward as a Northern man or as a Southern man. I am unwilling to recognize such divisions and distinctions. I have brought it forward as an American Senator, representing a State which is true to this principle, and which has approved of my action in respect to the Nebraska bill. I have brought it forward not as an act of justice to the South more than to the North. I have presented it especially as an act of justice to the people of those Territories and of the States to be formed therefrom, now and in all time to come. I have nothing to say about Northern rights or Southern rights. I know of no such divisions or distinctions under the Constitution. The bill does equal and exact justice to the whole Union, and every part of it; it violates the right of no State or Territory; but places each on a perfect equality, and leaves the people thereof to the free enjoyment of all their rights under the Constitution.

Now, sir, I wish to say to our Southern friends that if they desire to see this great principle carried out, now is their time to rally around it, to cherish it, preserve it, make it the rule of action in all future time. If they fail to do it now, and thereby allow the doctrine of interference to prevail, upon their heads the consequences of that interference must rest. To our Northern friends, on the other hand, I desire to say, that from this day henceforward they must rebuke the slander which has been uttered against the South, that they desire to legislate slavery into the Territories. The South has vindicated her sincerity, her honor, on that point by bringing forward a provision negativing, in express terms, any such effect as a result of this bill. I am rejoiced to know that while the proposition to abrogate the eighth section of the Missouri act comes from a free State, the proposition to negative the conclusion that slavery is thereby introduced, comes from a slave-holding State. Thus, both sides furnish conclusive evidence that they go for the principle, and the principle only, and desire to take no advantage of any possible misconstruction.

Mr. President, I feel that I owe an apology to the Senate for having occupied their attention so long, and a still greater apology for having discussed the question in such an incoherent and desultory manner. But I could not forbear to claim the right of closing this debate. I thought gentlemen would recognize its propriety when they saw the manner in which I was assailed and misrepresented in the course of this discussion, and especially by assaults still more disreputable in some portions of the country. These assaults have had no other effect upon me than to give me courage and energy for a still more resolute discharge of duty. I say frankly that, in my opinion, this measure will be as popular at the North as at the South, when its provisions and principles shall have been fully developed, and become well understood. The people at the North are attached to the principles of self-government, and you cannot convince them that that is self-government which deprives a people of the right of legislating for themselves, and compels them to receive laws which are forced upon them by a Legislature in which they are not represented. We are willing to stand upon this great principle of self-government everywhere; and it is to us a proud reflection that, in this whole discussion, no friend of the bill has urged an argument in its favor which could not be used with the same propriety in a free State as in a slave State, and *vice versâ*. No enemy of the bill has used an argument which would bear repetition one mile across Mason and Dixon's line. Our opponents have dealt entirely in sectional appeals. The friends of the bill have discussed a great principle of universal application, which can be sustained by the same reasons, and the same arguments, in every time and in every corner of the Union.

CHARLES SUMNER,

OF MASSACHUSETTS.

(BORN 1811, DIED 1874.)

ON THE CRIME AGAINST KANSAS; SENATE, MAY 19-20, 1856.

MR. PRESIDENT:

You are now called to redress a great transgression. Seldom in the history of nations has such a question been presented. Tariffs, Army bills, Navy bills, Land bills, are important, and justly occupy your care; but these all belong to the course of ordinary legislation. As means and instruments only, they are necessarily subordinate to the conservation of government itself. Grant them or deny them, in greater or less degree, and you will inflict no shock. The machinery of government will continue to move. The State will not cease to exist. Far otherwise is it with the eminent question now before you, involving, as it does, Liberty in a broad territory, and also involving the peace of the whole country, with our good name in history forever more.

Take down your map, sir, and you will find that the Territory of Kansas, more than any other region, occupies the middle spot of North America, equally distant from the Atlantic on the east, and the Pacific on the west; from the frozen waters of Hudson's Bay on the north, and the tepid Gulf Stream on the south, constituting the precise territorial centre of the whole vast continent. To such advantages of situation, on the very highway between two oceans, are added a soil of unsurpassed richness, and a fascinating, undulating beauty of surface, with a health-giving climate, calculated to nurture a powerful and generous people, worthy to be a central pivot of American institutions. A few short months only have passed since this spacious and mediterranean country was open only to the savage who ran wild in its woods and prairies; and now it has already drawn to its bosom a population of freemen larger than Athens crowded within her historic gates, when her sons, under Miltiades, won liberty for mankind on the field of Marathon; more than Sparta contained when she ruled Greece, and sent forth her devoted children, quickened by a mother's benediction, to return with their shields, or on them; more than Rome gathered on her seven hills, when, under her kings, she commenced that sovereign sway, which afterward embraced the whole earth ; more than London held, when, on the fields of Crecy and Agincourt, the English banner was carried victoriously over the chivalrous hosts of France.

Against this Territory, thus fortunate in position and population, a crime has been committed, which is without example in the records of the past. Not in plundered provinces or in the cruelties of selfish governors will you find its parallel; and yet there is an ancient instance, which may show at least the path of justice. In the terrible impeachment by which the great Roman orator has blasted through all time the name of Verres, amidst charges of robbery and sacrilege, the enormity which most aroused the indignant voice of his accuser, and which still stands forth with strongest distinctness, arresting the sympathetic indignation of all who read the story, is, that away in Sicily he had scourged a citizen of Rome—that the cry, " I am a Roman citizen," had been interposed in vain against the lash of the tyrant governor. Other charges were, that he had carried away productions of art, and that he had violated the sacred shrines. It was in the presence of the Roman Senate that this arraignment proceeded; in a temple of the Forum; amidst crowds—such as no orator had ever before drawn together—thronging the porticos and collonnades, even clinging to the house-tops and neighboring slopes—and under the anxious gaze of witnesses summoned from the scene of crime. But an audience grander far—of higher dignity—of more various people, and of wider intelligence—the countless multitude of succeeding generations, in every land, where eloquence has been studied, or where the Roman name has been recognized,—has listened to the accusation, and throbbed with condemnation of the criminal. Sir, speaking in an age of light, and a land of constitutional liberty, where the safeguards of elections are justly placed among the highest triumphs of civilization, I fearlessly assert that the wrongs of much-abused Sicily, thus memorable in history, were small by the side of the wrongs of Kansas, where the very shrines of popular institutions, more sacred than any heathen altar, have been desecrated; where the ballot-box, more precious than any work, in ivory or marble, from the cunning hand of art, has been plundered; and where the cry, "I am an American citizen," has been interposed in vain against outrage of every kind, even upon life itself. Are you against sacrilege? I present it for your execration. Are you against robbery? I hold it up to your scorn. Are you for the protection of American citizens? I show you how their dearest rights have been cloven down, while a Tyrannical Usurpation has sought to install itself on their very necks!

But the wickedness which I now begin to expose is immeasurably aggravated by the motive which prompted it. Not in any common lust for power did this uncommon tragedy have its origin. It is the rape of a virgin Territory, compelling it to the hateful embrace of Slavery; and it may be clearly traced to a depraved longing for a new slave State, the hideous offspring of such a crime, in the hope of adding to the power of slavery in the National Government. Yes, sir, when the whole world, alike Christian and Turk, is rising up to condemn this wrong, and to make it a hissing to the nations, here in our Republic, *force*—ay, sir, FORCE —has been openly employed in compelling Kansas to this pollution, and all for the sake of political power. There is the simple fact, which you will in vain attempt to deny, but which in itself presents an essential wickedness that makes other public crimes seem like public virtues.

But this enormity, vast beyond comparison, swells to dimensions of wickedness which the imagination toils in vain to grasp, when it is understood that for this purpose are hazarded the horrors of intestine feud not only in this distant Territory, but everywhere throughout the country. Already the muster has begun. The strife is no longer local, but national. Even now, while I speak, portents hang on all the arches of the horizon threatening to darken the broad land, which already yawns with the mutterings of civil war. The fury of the propagandists of Slavery, and the calm determination of their opponents, are now diffused from the distant Territory over widespread communities, and the whole country, in all its extent—marshalling hostile divisions, and foreshadowing a strife which, unless happily averted by the triumph of Freedom, will become war—fratricidal, parricidal war—with an accumulated wickedness beyond the wickedness of any war in human annals; justly provoking the avenging judgment of Providence and the avenging pen of history, and constituting a strife, in the language of the ancient writer, more than *foreign*, more than *social*, more than *civil*; but something compounded of all these strifes, and in itself more than war; *sed potius commune quoddam ex omnibus, et plus quam bellum.*

Such is the crime which you are to judge. But the criminal also must be dragged into day, that you may see and measure the power by which all this wrong is sustained. From no common source could it proceed. In its perpetration was needed a spirit of vaulting ambition which would hesitate at nothing; a hardihood of purpose which was insensible to the judgment of mankind; a madness for Slavery which would disregard the Constitution, the laws, and all the great examples of our history; also a consciousness of power such as comes from the habit of power; a combination of energies found only in a hundred arms directed by a hundred eyes; a control of public opinion through venal pens and a prostituted press; an ability to subsidize crowds in every vocation of life—the politician with his local importance, the lawyer with his subtle tongue, and even the authority of the judge on the bench; and a familiar use of men in places high and low, so that none, from the President to the lowest border postmaster, should decline to be its tool; all these things and more were needed, and they were found in the slave power of our Republic. There, sir, stands the criminal, all unmasked before you—heartless, grasping, and tyrannical—with an audacity beyond that of Verres, a subtlety beyond that of Machiavel, a meanness beyond that of Bacon, and an ability beyond that of Hastings. Justice to Kansas can be secured only by the prostration of this influence; for this the power behind—greater than any President—which succors and sustains the crime. Nay, the proceedings I now arraign derive their fearful consequences only from this connection.

In now opening this great matter, I am not insensible to the austere demands of the occasion; but the dependence of the crime against Kansas upon the slave power is so peculiar and important, that I trust to be pardoned while I impress it with an illustration, which to some may seem trivial. It is related in Northern mythology that the god of Force, visiting an enchanted region, was challenged by his royal entertainer to what seemed an humble feat of strength—merely, sir, to lift a cat from the ground. The god smiled at the challenge, and, calmly placing his hand under the belly of the animal, with superhuman strength strove, while the back of the feline monster arched far upward, even beyond reach, and one paw actually forsook the earth, until at last the discomfited divinity desisted; but he was little surprised at his defeat when he learned that this creature, which seemed to be a cat, and nothing more, was not merely a cat, but that it belonged to and was a part of the great Terrestrial Serpent, which, in its innumerable folds, encircled the whole globe. Even so the creature, whose paws are now fastened upon Kansas, whatever it may seem to be, constitutes in reality a part of the slave power, which, in its loathsome folds, is now coiled about the whole land. Thus do I expose the extent of the present contest, where we encounter not merely local resistance, but also the unconquered sustaining arm behind. But out of the vastness of the crime attempted, with all its woe and shame, I derive a well-founded assurance of a commensurate vastness of effort against it by the aroused masses of the country, determined not only to vindicate Right against Wrong, but to redeem the Republic from the thraldom of that Oligarchy which prompts, directs, and concentrates the distant wrong.

Such is the crime, and such the criminal, which it is my duty in this debate to expose, and, by the blessing of God, this duty shall be done completely to the end. * * *

But, before entering upon the argument, I must say something of a general character, particularly in response to what has fallen from Senators who have raised themselves to eminence on this floor in championship of human wrongs. I mean the Senator from South Carolina (Mr. Butler), and the Senator from Illinois (Mr. Douglas), who, though unlike as Don Quixote and Sancho Panza, yet, like this couple, sally forth together in the same adventure. I regret much to miss the elder Senator from his seat; but the cause, against which he has run a tilt, with such activity of animosity, demands that the opportunity of exposing him should not be lost; and it is for the cause that I speak. The Senator from South Carolina has read many books of chivalry, and believes himself a chivalrous knight, with sentiments of honor and courage. Of course he has chosen a mistress to whom he has made his vows, and who, though ugly to others, is always lovely to him; though polluted in the sight of the world, is chaste in his sight—I mean the harlot, Slavery. For her, his tongue is always profuse in words. Let her be impeached in character, or any proposition made to shut her out from the extension of her wantonness, and no extravagance of manner or hardihood of assertion is then too great for this Senator. The frenzy of Don Quixote, in behalf of his wench, Dulcinea del Toboso, is all surpassed. The asserted rights of Slavery, which shock equality of all kinds, are cloaked by a fantastic claim of equality. If the slave States cannot enjoy what, in mockery of the great fathers of the Republic, he misnames equality under the Constitution—in other words, the full power in the National Territories to compel fellow-men to unpaid toil, to separate husband and wife, and to sell little children at the auction block—then, sir, the chivalric Senator will conduct the State of South Carolina out of the Union! Heroic knight! Exalted Senator! A second Moses come for a second exodus!

But not content with this poor menace, which we have been twice told was "measured," the Senator in the unrestrained chivalry of his nature, has undertaken to apply opprobrious words to those who differ from him on this floor. He calls them "sectional and fanatical;" and opposition to the usurpation in Kansas he denounces as "an uncalculating fanaticism." To be sure these charges lack all grace of originality, and all sentiment of truth; but the adventurous Senator does not hesitate. He is the uncompromising, unblushing representative on this floor of a flagrant *sectionalism*, which now domineers over the Republic, and yet with a ludicrous ignorance of his own position— unable to see himself as others see him—or with an effrontery which even his white head ought not to protect from rebuke, he applies to those here who resist his *sectionalism* the very epithet which designates himself. The men who strive to bring back the Government to its original policy, when Freedom and not Slavery was sectional, he arraigns as *sectional*. This will not do. It involves too great a perversion of terms. I tell that Senator that it is to himself, and to the "organization" of which he is the "committed advocate," that this epithet belongs. I now fasten it upon them. For myself, I care little for names; but since the question has been raised here, I affirm that the

Republican party of the Union is in no just sense *sectional*, but, more than any other party, *national*; and that it now goes forth to dislodge from the high places of the Government the tyrannical sectionalism of which the Senator from South Carolina is one of the maddest zealots. * * *

As the Senator from South Carolina, is the Don Quixote, the Senator from Illinois (Mr. Douglas) is the Squire of Slavery, its very Sancho Panza, ready to do all its humiliating offices. This Senator, in his labored address, vindicating his labored report—piling one mass of elaborate error upon another mass—constrained himself, as you will remember, to unfamiliar decencies of speech. Of that address I have nothing to say at this moment, though before I sit down I shall show something of its fallacies. But I go back now to an earlier occasion, when, true to his native impulses, he threw into this discussion, "for a charm of powerful trouble," personalities most discreditable to this body. I will not stop to repel the imputations which he cast upon myself; but I mention them to remind you of the "sweltered venom sleeping got," which, with other poisoned ingredients, he cast into the caldron of this debate. Of other things I speak. Standing on this floor, the Senator issued his rescript, requiring submission to the Usurped Power of Kansas; and this was accompanied by a manner—all his own—such as befits the tyrannical threat. Very well. Let the Senator try. I tell him now that he cannot enforce any such submission. The Senator, with the slave power at his back, is strong; but he is not strong enough for this purpose. He is bold. He shrinks from nothing. Like Danton, he may cry, "*l'audace! l'audace! toujours l'audace!*" but even his audacity cannot compass this work. The Senator copies the British officer who, with boastful swagger, said that with the hilt of his sword he would cram the "stamps" down the throats of the American people, and he will meet a similar failure. He may convulse this country with a civil feud. Like the ancient madman, he may set fire to this Temple of Constitutional Liberty, grander than the Ephesian dome; but he cannot enforce obedience to that Tyrannical Usurpation.

The Senator dreams that he can subdue the North. He disclaims the open threat, but his conduct still implies it. How little that Senator knows himself or the strength of the cause which he persecutes! He is but a mortal man; against him is an immortal principle. With finite power he wrestles with the infinite, and he must fall. Against him are stronger battalions than any marshalled by mortal arm—the inborn, ineradicable, invincible sentiments of the human heart; against him is nature in all her subtle forces; against him is God. Let him try to subdue these. * * *

With regret, I come again upon the Senator from South Carolina (Mr. Butler), who, omnipresent in this debate, overflowed with rage at the simple suggestion that Kansas had applied for admission as a State; and, with incoherent phrases, discharged the loose expectoration of his speech, now upon her representative, and then upon her people. There was no extravagance of the ancient parliamentary debate, which he did not repeat; nor was there any possible deviation from truth which he did not make, with so much of passion, I am glad to add, as to save him from the suspicion of intentional aberration. But the Senator touches nothing which he does not disfigure—with error, sometimes of principle, sometimes of fact. He shows an incapacity of accuracy, whether in stating the Constitution, or in stating the law, whether in the details of statistics or the diversions of scholarship. He cannot ope his mouth, but out there flies a blunder. Surely he ought to be familiar with the life of Franklin; and yet he referred to this household character, while acting as agent of our fathers in England, as above suspicion; and this was done that he might give point to a false contrast with the agent of Kansas—not knowing that, however they may differ in genius and fame, in this experience they are alike: that Franklin, when entrusted with the petition of Massachusetts Bay, was assaulted by a foul-mouthed speaker, where he could not be heard in defence, and denounced as a "thief," even as the agent of Kansas has been assaulted on this floor, and denounced as a "forger." And let not the vanity of the Senator be inspired by the parallel with the British statesman of that day; for it is only in hostility to Freedom that any parallel can be recognized.

But it is against the people of Kansas that the sensibilities of the Senator are particularly aroused. Coming, as he announces, "from a State"—ay, sir, from South Carolina—he turns with lordly disgust from this newly-formed community, which he will not recognize even as a "body politic." Pray, sir, by what title does he indulge in this egotism? Has he read the history of "the State" which he represents? He cannot surely have forgotten its shameful imbecility from Slavery, confessed throughout the Revolution, followed by its more shameful assumptions for Slavery since. He cannot have forgotten its wretched persistence in the slave-trade as the very apple of its eye, and the condition of its participation in the Union. He cannot have forgotten its constitution, which is Republican only in name, confirming power in the hands of the few, and founding the qualifications of its legislators on "a settled freehold estate and ten negroes." And yet the Senator, to whom that "State" has in part committed the guardianship of its good name, instead of moving, with backward treading steps, to cover its nakedness, rushes forward in the very ecstasy of madness, to expose it by provoking a comparison with Kansas. South Carolina is old; Kansas is young. South Carolina counts by centuries; where Kansas counts by years. But a beneficent example may be born in a day; and I venture to say, that against the two centuries of the older "State," may be already set the two years of trial, evolving corresponding virtue, in the younger community. In the one, is the long wail of Slavery; in the other, the hymns of Freedom. And if we glance at special achievements, it will be difficult to find any thing in the history of South Carolina which presents so much of heroic spirit in an heroic cause as appears in that repulse of the Missouri invaders by the beleaguered town of Lawrence, where even the women gave their effective efforts to Freedom. The matrons of Rome, who poured their jewels into the treasury for the public defence—the wives of Prussia, who, with delicate fingers, clothed their defenders against French invasion—the mothers of our own Revolution, who sent forth their sons, covered with prayers and blessings, to combat for human rights, did nothing of self-sacrifice truer than did these women on this occasion. Were the whole history of South Carolina blotted out of existence, from its very beginning down to the day of the last election of the Senator to his present seat on this floor, civilization might lose—I do not say how little; but surely less than it has already gained by the example of Kansas, in its valiant struggle against oppression, and in the development of a new science of emigration. Already, in Lawrence alone, there are newspapers and schools, including a High School, and throughout this infant Territory there is more mature scholarship far, in proportion to its inhabitants, than in all South Carolina. Ah, sir, I tell the Senator that Kansas, welcomed as a free State, will be a "ministering angel" to the Republic, when South Carolina, in the cloak of darkness which she hugs, "lies howling."

The Senator from Illinois (Mr. Douglas) naturally joins the Senator from South Carolina in this warfare, and gives to it the superior intensity of his nature. He thinks that the National Government has not completely proved its power, as it has never hanged a traitor; but, if the occasion requires, he hopes there will be no hesitation; and this threat is directed at Kansas, and even at the friends of Kansas throughout the country. Again occurs the parallel with the struggle of our fathers, and I borrow the language of Patrick Henry, when, to the cry from the Senator, of "treason," "treason," I reply, " if this be treason, make the most of it." Sir, it is easy to call names; but I beg to tell the Senator that if the word "traitor" is in any way applicable to those who refuse submission to a Tyrannical

Usurpation, whether in Kansas or elsewhere, then must some new word, of deeper color, be invented, to designate those mad spirits who could endanger and degrade the Republic, while they betray all the cherished sentiments of the fathers and the spirit of the Constitution, in order to give new spread to Slavery. Let the Senator proceed. It will not be the first time in history, that a scaffold erected for punishment has become a pedestal of honor. Out of death comes life, and the "traitor" whom he blindly executes will live immortal in the cause.

"For Humanity sweeps onward; where to-day the martyr stands,
On the morrow crouches Judas, with the silver in his hands;
While the hooting mob of yesterday in silent awe return,
To glean up the scattered ashes into History's golden urn."

Among these hostile Senators, there is yet another, with all the prejudices of the Senator from South Carolina, but without his generous impulses, who, on account of his character before the country, and the rancor of his opposition, deserves to be named. I mean the Senator from Virginia (Mr. Mason), who, as the author of the Fugitive-Slave bill, has associated himself with a special act of inhumanity and tyranny. Of him I shall say little, for he has said little in this debate, though within that little was compressed the bitterness of a life absorbed in the support of Slavery. He holds the commission of Virginia; but he does not represent that early Virginia, so dear to our hearts, which gave to us the pen of Jefferson, by which the equality of men was declared, and the sword of Washington, by which Independence was secured; but he represents that other Virginia, from which Washington and Jefferson now avert their faces, where human beings are bred as cattle for the shambles, and where a dungeon rewards the pious matron who teaches little children to relieve their bondage by reading the Book of Life. It is proper that such a Senator, representing such a State, should rail against free Kansas.

Senators such as these are the natural enemies of Kansas, and I introduce them with reluctance, simply that the country may understand the character of the hostility which must be overcome. Arrayed with them, of course, are all who unite, under any pretext or apology, in the propagandism of human Slavery. To such, indeed, the time-honored safeguards of popular rights can be a name only, and nothing more. What are trial by jury, habeas corpus, the ballot-box, the right of petition, the liberty of Kansas, your liberty, sir, or mine, to one who lends himself, not merely to the support at home, but to the propagandism abroad, of that preposterous wrong, which denies even the right of a man to himself! Such a cause can be maintained only by a practical subversion of all rights. It is, therefore, merely according to reason that its partisans should uphold the Usurpation in Kansas.

To overthrow this Usurpation is now the special, importunate duty of Congress, admitting of no hesitation or postponement. To this end it must lift itself from the cabals of candidates, the machinations of party, and the low level of vulgar strife. It must turn from that Slave Oligarchy which now controls the Republic, and refuse to be its tool. Let its power be stretched forth toward this distant Territory, not to bind, but to unbind; not for the oppression of the weak, but for the subversion of the tyrannical; not for the prop and maintenance of a revolting Usurpation, but for the confirmation of Liberty.

"These are imperial arts and worthy thee!"

Let it now take its stand between the living and dead, and cause this plague to be stayed. All this it can do; and if the interests of Slavery did not oppose, all this it would do at once, in reverent regard for justice, law, and order, driving away all the alarms of war; nor would it dare to brave the shame and punishment of this great refusal. But the slave power dares any thing; and it can be conquered only by the united masses of the people. From Congress to the People I appeal. * * *

The contest, which, beginning in Kansas, has reached us, will soon be transferred from Congress to a broader stage, where every citizen will be not only spectator, but actor; and to their judgment I confidently appeal. To the People, now on the eve of exercising the electoral franchise, in choosing a Chief Magistrate of the Republic, I appeal, to vindicate the electoral franchise in Kansas. Let the ballot-box of the Union, with multitudinous might, protect the ballot-box in that Territory. Let the voters everywhere, while rejoicing in their own rights, help to guard the equal rights of distant fellow-citizens; that the shrines of popular institutions, now desecrated, may be sanctified anew; that the ballot-box, now plundered, may be restored; and that the cry, "I am an American citizen," may not be sent forth in vain against outrage of every kind. In just regard for free labor in that Territory, which it is sought to blast by unwelcome association with slave labor; in Christian sympathy with the slave, whom it is proposed to task and sell there; in stern condemnation of the crime which has been consummated on that beautiful soil; in rescue of fellow-citizens now subjugated to a Tyrannical Usurpation; in dutiful respect for the early fathers, whose aspirations are now ignobly thwarted; in the name of the Constitution, which has been outraged—of the laws trampled down—of Justice banished—of Humanity degraded—of Peace destroyed—of Freedom crushed to earth; and, in the name of the Heavenly Father, whose service is perfect Freedom, I make this last appeal.

May 20, 1856.

MR. DOUGLAS:—I shall not detain the Senate by a detailed reply to the speech of the Senator from Massachusetts. Indeed, I should not deem it necessary to say one word, but for the personalities in which he has indulged, evincing a depth of malignity that issued from every sentence, making it a matter of self-respect with me to repel the assaults which have been made.

As to the argument, we have heard it all before. Not a position, not a fact, not an argument has he used, which has not been employed on the same side of the chamber, and replied to by me twice. I shall not follow him, therefore, because it would only be repeating the same answer which I have twice before given to each of his positions. He seems to get up a speech as in Yankee land they get up a bedquilt. They take all the old calico dresses of various colors, that have been in the house from the days of their grandmothers, and invite the young ladies of the neighborhood in the afternoon, and the young men to meet them at a dance in the evening. They cut up these pieces of old dresses and make pretty figures, and boast of what beautiful ornamental work they have made, although there was not a new piece of material in the whole quilt. Thus it is with the speech which we have had rehashed here to-day, in regard to matters of fact, matters of law, and matters of argument—every thing but the personal assaults and the malignity. * * *

His endeavor seems to be an attempt to whistle to keep up his courage by defiant assaults upon us all. I am in doubt as to what can be his object. He has not hesitated to charge three fourths of the Senate with fraud, with swindling, with crime, with infamy, at least one hundred times over in his speech. Is it his object to provoke some of us to kick him as we would a dog in the street, that he may get sympathy upon the just chastisement? What is the object of this denunciation against the body of which we are members? A hundred times he has called the Nebraska bill a "swindle," an act of crime, an act of infamy, and each time went on to illustrate the complicity of each man who voted for it in perpetrating the crime. He has brought it home as a personal charge to those who passed the Nebraska bill, that they were guilty of a crime which deserved the just indignation of heaven, and should make them infamous among men.

Who are the Senators thus arraigned? He does me the honor to make me the chief. It was my good luck to have such a position in this body as to enable me to be the author of a great, wise measure, which the Senate has approved, and the country will endorse. That measure was sustained by about three fourths of all the members of the Senate. It was sustained by a majority of the Democrats and a majority of the Whigs in this body. It was sustained by a majority of Senators from the slave-holding States, and a majority of Senators from the free States. The Senator, by his charge of crime, then, stultifies three fourths of the whole body, a majority of the North, nearly the whole South, a majority of Whigs, and a majority of Democrats here. He says they are infamous. If he so believed, who could suppose that he would ever show his face among such a body of men? How dare he approach one of those gentlemen to give him his hand after that act? If he felt the courtesies between men he would not do it. He would deserve to have himself spit in the face for doing so. * * *

The attack of the Senator from Massachusetts now is not on me alone. Even the courteous and the accomplished Senator from South Carolina (Mr. Butler) could not be passed by in his absence.

MR. MASON:—Advantage was taken of it.

MR. DOUGLAS:—It is suggested that advantage is taken of his absence. I think that this is a mistake. I think the speech was written and practised, and the gestures fixed; and, if that part had been stricken out the Senator would not have known how to repeat the speech. All that tirade of abuse must be brought down on the head of the venerable, the courteous, and the distinguished Senator from South Carolina. I shall not defend that gentleman here. Every Senator who knows him loves him. The Senator from Massachusetts may take every charge made against him in his speech, and may verify by his oath, and by the oath of every one of his confederates, and there is not an honest man in this chamber who will not repel it as a slander. Your oaths cannot make a Senator feel that it was not an outrage to assail that honorable gentleman in the terms in which he has been attacked. He, however, will be here in due time to speak for himself, and to act for himself too. I know what will happen. The Senator from Massachusetts will go to him, whisper a secret apology in his ear, and ask him to accept that as satisfaction for a public outrage on his character! I know the Senator from Massachusetts is in the habit of doing those things. I have had some experience of his skill in that respect. * * *

Why these attacks on individuals by name, and two thirds of the Senate collectively? Is it the object to drive men here to dissolve social relations with political opponents? Is it to turn the Senate into a bear garden, where Senators cannot associate on terms which ought to prevail between gentlemen? These attacks are heaped upon me by man after man. When I repel them, it is intimated that I show some feeling on the subject. Sir, God grant that when I denounce an act of infamy I shall do it with feeling, and do it under the sudden impulses of feeling, instead of sitting up at night writing out my denunciation of a man whom I hate, copying it, having it printed, punctuating the proof-sheets, and repeating it before the glass, in order to give refinement to insult, which is only pardonable when it is the outburst of a just indignation.

Mr. President, I shall not occupy the time of the Senate. I dislike to be forced to repel these attacks upon myself, which seem to be repeated on every occasion. It appears that gentlemen on the other side of the chamber think they would not be doing justice to their cause if they did not make myself a personal object of bitter denunciation and malignity. I hope that the debate on this bill may be brought to a close at as early a day as possible. I shall do no more in these side discussions than vindicate myself and repel unjust attacks, but I shall ask the Senate to permit me to close the debate, when it shall close, in a calm, kind summary of the whole question, avoiding personalities.

MR. SUMNER:—Mr. President, To the Senator from Illinois, I should willingly leave the privilege of the common scold—the last word; but I will not leave to him, in any discussion with me, the last argument, or the last semblance of it. He has crowned the audacity of this debate by venturing to rise here and calumniate me. He said that I came here, took an oath to support the Constitution, and yet determined not to support a particular clause in that Constitution. To that statement I give, to his face, the flattest denial. When it was made on a former occasion on this floor by the absent Senator from South Carolina (Mr. Butler), I then repelled it. I will read from the debate of the 28th of June, 1854, as published in the *Globe*, to show what I said in response to that calumny when pressed at that hour. Here is what I said to the Senator from South Carolina:

"This Senator was disturbed, when to his inquiry, personally, pointedly, and vehemently addressed to me, whether I would join in returning a fellow-man to slavery? I exclaimed, 'Is thy servant a dog, that he should do this thing?'"

You will observe that the inquiry of the Senator from South Carolina, was whether I would join in returning a fellow-man to slavery. It was not whether I would support any clause of the Constitution of the United States—far from that. * * *

Sir, this is the Senate of the United States, an important body, under the Constitution, with great powers. Its members are justly supposed, from age, to be above the intemperance of youth, and from character to be above the gusts of vulgarity. They are supposed to have something of wisdom, and something of that candor which is the handmaid of wisdom. Let the Senator bear these things in mind, and let him remember hereafter that the bowie-knife and bludgeon are not the proper emblems of Senatorial debate. Let him remember that the swagger of Bob Acres and the ferocity of the Malay cannot add dignity to this body. The Senator has gone on to infuse into his speech the venom which has been sweltering for months—ay, for years; and he has alleged facts that are entirely without foundation, in order to heap upon me some personal obloquy. I will not go into the details which have flowed out so naturally from his tongue. I only brand them to his face as false. I say, also, to that Senator, and I wish him to bear it in mind, that no person with the upright form of man can be allowed—(Hesitation.)

MR. DOUGLAS:—Say it.

MR. SUMNER:—I will say it—no person with the upright form of man can be allowed, without violation to all decency, to switch out from his tongue the perpetual stench of offensive personality. Sir, that is not a proper weapon of debate, at least, on this floor. The noisome, squat, and nameless animal, to which I now refer, is not a proper model for an American Senator. Will the Senator from Illinois take notice?

MR. DOUGLAS:—I will; and therefore will not imitate you, sir.

MR. SUMNER:—I did not hear the Senator.

MR. DOUGLAS:—I said if that be the case I would certainly never imitate you in that capacity, recognizing the force of the illustration.

MR. SUMNER:—Mr. President, again the Senator has switched his tongue, and again he fills the Senate with its offensive odor. * * *

MR. DOUGLAS:—I am not going to pursue

this subject further. I will only say that a man who has been branded by me in the Senate, and convicted by the Senate of falsehood, cannot use language requiring a reply, and therefore I have nothing more to say.

PRESTON S. BROOKS,

OF SOUTH CAROLINA.

(BORN 1819, DIED 1857.)

ON THE SUMNER ASSAULT; HOUSE OF REPRESENTATIVES, JULY 14, 1856.

MR. SPEAKER:

Some time since a Senator from Massachusetts allowed himself, in an elaborately prepared speech, to offer a gross insult to my State, and to a venerable friend, who is my State representative, and who was absent at the time.

Not content with that, he published to the world, and circulated extensively, this uncalled-for libel on my State and my blood. Whatever insults my State insults me. Her history and character have commanded my pious veneration; and in her defence I hope I shall always be prepared, humbly and modestly, to perform the duty of a son. I should have forfeited my own self-respect, and perhaps the good opinion of my countrymen, if I had failed to resent such an injury by calling the offender in question to a personal account. It was a personal affair, and in taking redress into my own hands I meant no disrespect to the Senate of the United States or to this House. Nor, sir, did I design insult or disrespect to the State of Massachusetts. I was aware of the personal responsibilities I incurred, and was willing to meet them. I knew, too, that I was amenable to the laws of the country, which afford the same protection to all, whether they be members of Congress or private citizens. I did not, and do not now believe, that I could be properly punished, not only in a court of law, but here also, at the pleasure and discretion of the House. I did not then, and do not now, believe that the spirit of American freemen would tolerate slander in high places, and permit a member of Congress to publish and circulate a libel on another, and then call upon either House to protect him against the personal responsibilities which he had thus incurred.

But if I had committed a breach of privilege, it was the privilege of the Senate, and not of this House, which was violated. I was answerable *there*, and not *here*. They had no right, as it seems to me, to prosecute me in these Halls, nor have you the right in law or under the Constitution, as I respectfully submit, to take jurisdiction over offences committed against them. The Constitution does not justify them in making such a request, nor this House in granting it. If, unhappily, the day should ever come when sectional or party feeling should run so high as to control all other considerations of public duty or justice, how easy it will be to use such precedents for the excuse of arbitrary power, in either House, to expel members of the minority who may have rendered themselves obnoxious to the prevailing spirit in the House to which they belong.

Matters may go smoothly enough when one House asks the other to punish a member who is offensive to a majority of its own body; but how will it be when, upon a pretence of insulted dignity, *demands* are made of this House to expel a member who happens to run counter to its party predilections, or other demands which it may not be so agreeable to grant? It could never have been designed by the Constitution of the United States to expose the two Houses to such temptations to collision, or to extend so far the discretionary power which was given to either House to punish its own members for the violation of its rules and orders. Discretion has been said to be the law of the tyrant, and when exercised under the color of the law, and under the influence of party dictation, it may and will become a terrible and insufferable despotism.

This House, however, it would seem, from the unmistakable tendency of its proceedings, takes a different view from that which I deliberately entertain in common with many others.

So far as public interests or constitutional rights are involved, I have now exhausted my means of defence. I may, then, be allowed to take a more personal view of the question at issue. The further prosecution of this subject, in the shape it has now assumed, may not only involve my friends, but the House itself, in agitations which might be unhappy in their consequences to the country. If these consequences could be confined to myself individually, I think I am prepared and ready to meet them, here or elsewhere; and when I use this language I mean what I say. But others must not suffer for me. I have felt more on account of my two friends who have been implicated, than for myself, for they have proven that "there is a friend that sticketh closer than a brother." I will not constrain gentlemen to assume a responsibility on my account, which possibly they would not run on their own.

Sir, I cannot, on *my own account*, assume the responsibility, in the face of the American people, of commencing a line of conduct which in my heart of hearts I believe would result in subverting the foundations of this Government, and in drenching this Hall in blood. No act of mine, on my personal account, shall inaugurate revolution; but when you, Mr. Speaker, return to your own home, and hear the people of the great North—and they are a great people—speak of me as a bad man, you will do me the justice to say that a blow struck by me at this time would be followed by revolution—and this I know. (Applause and hisses in the gallery.)

Mr. Brooks (resuming):—If I desired to kill the Senator, why did not I do it? You all admit that I had him in my power. Let me tell the member from New Jersey that it was expressly to avoid taking life that I used an ordinary cane, presented to me by a friend in Baltimore, nearly three months before its application to the "bare head" of the Massachusetts Senator. I went to work very deliberately, as I am charged—and this is admitted,—and speculated somewhat as to whether I should employ a horsewhip or a cowhide; but knowing that the Senator was my superior in strength, it occurred to me that he might wrest it from my hand, and then—for I never attempt any thing I do not perform—I might have been compelled to do that which I would have regretted the balance of my natural life.

The question has been asked in certain newspapers, why I did not invite the Senator to personal combat in the mode usually adopted. Well, sir, as I desire the whole truth to be known about the matter, I will for once notice a newspaper article on the floor of the House, and answer here.

My answer is, that the Senator would not accept a message; and having formed the unalterable determination to punish him, I believed that the offence of "sending a hostile message," superadded to the indictment for assault and battery, would subject me to legal penalties more severe than would be imposed for a simple assault and battery. That is my answer.

Now, Mr. Speaker, I have nearly finished what I intended to say. If my opponents, who have pursued me with unparalleled bitterness, are satisfied with the present condition of this affair, I am. I return my thanks to my friends, and especially to those who are from non-slave-owning States, who have magnanimously sustained me, and felt that it was a higher honor to themselves to be just in their judgment of a gentleman than to be a member of Congress for life. In taking my leave, I feel that it is proper that I should say that I believe that some of the votes that have been cast against me have been extorted by an outside pressure at home, and that their votes do not express the feelings or opinions of the members who gave them.

To such of these as have given their votes and made their speeches on the constitutional principles involved, and without indulging in personal vilification, I owe my respect. But, sir, they have written me down upon the history of the country as worthy of expulsion, and in no unkindness I must tell them that for all future time my self-respect requires that I shall pass them as strangers.

And now, Mr. Speaker, I announce to you

and to this House, that I am no longer a member of the Thirty-Fourth Congress.

(Mr. Brooks then walked out of the House of Representatives.)

ANSON BURLINGAME,

OF MASSACHUSETTS.

(BORN 1822, DIED 1873.)

IN DEFENCE OF MASSACHUSETTS; HOUSE OF REPRESENTATIVES, JUNE 21, 1856.

MR. CHAIRMAN:

The House will bear me witness that I have not pressed myself upon its deliberations. I never before asked its indulgence. I have assailed no man; nor have I sought to bring reproach upon any man's State. But, while such has been my course, as well as the course of my colleagues from Massachusetts, upon this floor, certain members have seen fit to assail the State which we represent, not only with words, but with blows.

In remembrance of these things, and seizing the first opportunity which has presented itself for a long time, I stand here to-day to say a word for old Massachusetts—not that she needs it; no, sir; for in all that constitutes true greatness—in all that gives abiding strength—in great qualities of head and of heart—in moral power—in material prosperity—in intellectual resources and physical ability—by the general judgment of mankind, according to her population, she is the first State. There does not live the man anywhere, who knows any thing, to whom praise of Massachusetts would not be needless. She is as far beyond that as she is beyond censure. Members here may sneer at her expense—they may praise her past at the expense of her present; but I say, with a full conviction of its truth, that Massachusetts, in her present performances, is even greater than in her past recollections. And when I have said this, what more can I say?

Sir, although I am here as her youngest and humblest member, yet, as her Representative, I feel that I am the peer of any man upon this floor. Occupying that high stand-point, with modesty, but with firmness, I cast down her glove to the whole band of her assailants.

She has been assailed in the House and out of the House, at the other end of the Capitol and at the other end of the avenue. There have been brought against her general charges and specific charges. I am sorry to find at the head of her assailants the President of the United States, who not only assails Massachusetts but the whole North. * * *

But, Mr. Chairman, all these assaults upon the State of Massachusetts sink into insignificance, compared with the one I am about to mention. On the 19th of May, it was announced that Mr. SUMNER would address the Senate upon the Kansas question. The floor of the Senate, the galleries, and avenues leading thereto, were thronged with an expectant audience; and many of us left our places in this House to hear the Massachusetts orator. To say that we were delighted with the speech we heard, would but faintly express the deep emotions of our hearts awakened by it. I need not speak of the classic purity of its language, nor of the nobility of its sentiments. It was heard by many; it has been read by millions. There has been no such speech made in the Senate since the days when those Titans of American eloquence—the Websters and the Haynes—contended with each other for mastery.

It was severe, because it was launched against tyranny. It was severe as Chatham was severe when he defended the feeble colonies against the giant oppression of the mother country. It was made in the face of a hostile Senate. It continued through the greater portion of two days; and yet, during that time, the speaker was not once called to order. This fact is conclusive as to the personal and parliamentary decorum of the speech. He had provocation enough. His State had been called hypocritical. He himself had been called "a puppy," "a fool," "a fanatic," and "a dishonest man." Yet he was parliamentary from the beginning to the end of his speech. No man knew better than he did the proprieties of the place, for he had always observed them. No man knew better than he did parliamentary law, because he had made it the study of his life. No man saw more clearly than he did the flaming sword of the Constitution, turning every way, guarding all the avenues of the Senate. But he was not thinking of these things; he was not thinking then of the privileges of the Senate nor of the guaranties of the Constitution; he was there to denounce tyranny and crime, and he did it. He was there to speak for the rights of an empire, and he did it, bravely and grandly.

So much for the occasion of the speech. A

word, and I shall be pardoned, about the speaker himself. He is my friend; for many and many a year I have looked to him for guidance and light, and I never looked in vain. He never had a personal enemy in his life; his character is as pure as the snow that falls on his native hills; his heart overflows with kindness for every being having the upright form of man; he is a ripe scholar, a chivalric gentleman, and a warm-hearted, true friend. He sat at the feet of Channing, and drank in the sentiments of that noble soul. He bathed in the learning and undying love of the great jurist Story; and the hand of Jackson, with its honors and its offices, sought him early in life, but he shrank from them with instinctive modesty. Sir, he is the pride of Massachusetts. His mother commonwealth found him adorning the highest walks of literature and law, and she bade him go and grace somewhat the rough character of political life. The people of Massachusetts—the old and the young and the middle-aged, now pay their full homage to the beauty of his public and private character. Such is CHARLES SUMNER.

On the 22d day of May, when the Senate and the House had clothed themselves in mourning for a brother fallen in the battle of life in the distant State of Missouri, the Senator from Massachusetts sat in the silence of the Senate chamber, engaged in the employments pertaining to his office, when a member from this House, who had taken an oath to sustain the Constitution, stole into the Senate, that place which had hitherto been held sacred against violence, and smote him as Cain smote his brother.

Mr. KEITT (in his seat):—That is false.

Mr. BURLINGAME:—I will not bandy epithets with the gentleman. I am responsible for my own language. Doubtless he is responsible for his.

Mr. KEITT:—I am.

Mr. BURLINGAME:—I shall stand by mine. One blow was enough; but it did not satiate the wrath of that spirit which had pursued him through two days. Again and again, quicker and faster fell the leaden blows, until he was torn away from his victim, when the Senator from Massachusetts fell in the arms of his friends, and his blood ran down on the Senate floor. Sir, the act was brief, and my comments on it shall be brief also. I denounce it in the name of the Constitution it violated. I denounce it in the name of the sovereignty of

Massachusetts, which was stricken down by the blow. I denounce it in the name of humanity. I denounce it in the name of civilization which it outraged. I denounce it in the name of that fair-play which bullies and prize-fighters respect. What! strike a man when he is pinioned—when he cannot respond to a blow? Call you that chivalry? In what code of honor did you get your authority for that? I do not believe that member has a friend so dear who must not, in his heart of hearts, condemn the act. Even the member himself, if he has left a spark of that chivalry and gallantry attributed to him, must loathe and scorn the act. God knows I do not wish to speak unkindly, or in a spirit of revenge; but I owe it to my manhood and the noble State I, in part, represent, to express my abhorrence of the act. But much as I reprobate the act, much more do I reprobate the conduct of those who were by, and saw the outrage perpetrated. Sir, especially do I notice the conduct of that Senator recently from the free platform of Massachusetts, with the odor of her hospitality on him, who stood there, not only silent and quiet while it was going on, but, when it was over, approved the act. And worse; when he had time to cool, when he had slept on it, he went into the Senate chamber of the United States, and shocked the sensibilities of the world by approving it. Another Senator did not take part because he feared that his motives might be questioned, exhibiting as extraordinary a delicacy as that individual who refused to rescue a drowning mortal because he had not been introduced to him. Another was not on good terms; and yet, if rumor be true, that Senator has declared that himself and family are more indebted to Mr. Sumner than to any other man; yet, when he saw him borne bleeding by, he turned and went on the other side. Oh, magnanimous SLIDELL! Oh, prudent DOUGLAS! Oh, audacious TOOMBS!

Sir, there are questions arising out of this which far transcend those of a mere personal nature. Of those personal considerations I shall speak, when the question comes properly before us, if I am permitted to do so. The higher question involves the very existence of the Government itself. If, sir, freedom of speech is not to remain to us, what is all this Government worth? If we from Massachusetts, or any other State—Senators, or members of the House—are to be called to account by some "gallant nephew" of some "gallant uncle," when we utter something which does not suit their sensitive natures, we desire to know it. If the conflict is to be transferred from this peaceful, intellectual field to one where, it is said, "honors are easy and responsibilities equal," then we desire to know it. Massachusetts, if her sons and representatives are to have the rod held over them, if these things are to continue, the time may come—though she utters no threats—when she may be called upon to withdraw them to her own bosom, where she can furnish to them that protection which is not vouchsafed to them under the flag of their common country. But, while she permits us to remain, we shall do our duty—our whole duty. We shall speak whatever we choose to speak, when we will, where we will, and how we will, regardless of all consequences.

Sir, the sons of Massachusetts are educated at the knees of their mothers, in the doctrines of peace and good-will, and, God knows, they desire to cultivate those feelings—feelings of social kindness, and public kindness. The House will bear witness that we have not violated or trespassed upon any of them; but, sir, if we are pushed too long and too far, there are men from the old commonwealth of Massachusetts who will not shrink from a defence of freedom of speech, and the honored State they represent, on any field where they may be assailed.

THOMAS L. CLINGMAN,

OF NORTH CAROLINA.

(BORN 1813.)

ON "DEBATES" IN CONGRESS; HOUSE OF REPRESENTATIVES, JULY 9, 1856.

MR. SPEAKER:

If on the present occasion any gentleman desires to get into difficulty, and is gratified in his wishes, I hope we shall not have a great howl in any part of the country over it. I hope that it will be looked upon as a mere personal matter for the gratification of the gentlemen who engage in it. And as I am a peaceable man, and never like to get into difficulties, so I do not take much pains to get out of their way; and as, during this hot weather, I feel very languid and indisposed to exertion, I shall not take especial pains to get out of the way of anybody who may be in search of such a thing. While I do not intend to utter any thing to offend any gentleman who does not want to be offended, still, if any one upon this floor—I limit the remarks to members of the House, not extending it to outsiders at all—wants a difficulty with me on this subject, I am perfectly willing for him to take it for granted that I have insulted him, and am responsible in any manner that he desires; but if he does not desire it, then not for the world would I offend him. But if this is to be a matter of mere abuse and vituperation, I wash my hands of it; I do not intend to embark in any thing of that kind. I regard fighting as objectionable in many respects, but quarrelling and denunciation are vastly more intolerable. When the British made war on China, the Chinese went into the field armed with gongs, and made a terrible noise, to induce the English, doubtless, to leave their territory. So if this is to be a mere Chinese gong business—an effort, in other words, to see who can make the loudest and most disagreeable noise, I will keep clear of it, and, if necessary, put my fingers in my ears to escape its annoyance.

And now let me call the attention of the House to the case under consideration. As I have already said, it is one which has produced a very great and remarkable excitement in the country. This, Mr. Speaker, may well be a matter of surprise to me; for though I have not been here a great many years as a member, yet about a dozen collisions on the floors of the two Houses have occurred in my time, and they were much stronger cases than this, because they took place while the Houses were in session. Why, I recollect that, during my first Congress, Mr. White of Kentucky and Mr. Rathbun of New York had a set-to just near where I now stand, during a period of great excitement, and when politics ran very high, with reference to a personally offensive charge against Mr. Clay; but the House never adopted any proceedings against those members, and it made no noise in the country. I recollect, too, that, in the next Congress, a gentleman from Georgia and another from Tennessee had a struggle over on the other side of the chamber, and several large desks were overturned, and the gentlemen apologized for disturbing our deliberations; but the House did not raise any committee, or censure them in any wise. Also, toward the close of that session, whilst the House was in session, at a late hour in the night, during a sort of triangular fight, a gentleman from Alabama struck a gentleman from the Northwest over the head with a cane, and cut it so that it bled very freely; but this did not cause the raising of any committee, or any other proceeding against the parties. I remember, too, going into the Senate that night, near one or two o'clock—and I must say here, that these disturbances occur more frequently during the last night of the session, when gentlemen, having been up for two or three days and nights successively, have gotten sleepy, and those who are in the habit of drinking spirits, drink a little from patriotic motives, just to keep awake, so as to be able to attend to the public business.

But, as I was saying, I went into the Senate chamber that night, and a Senator asked me what we had been doing in the House? I replied that we had just had a little fight there among three of the members. "Why," said he, with an air of exultation, "we have had two in the Senate to-night!" and it was true. It was on that occasion that a Senator from Pennsylvania was standing up making a speech, and a Senator from Mississippi, not liking his speech, went up and struck him in the face, or attemptted so to strike him, and they had a regular set-to. The Senate, however, did not raise any committee to take charge of the subject.

During the next Congress two members from

North Carolina had a collision just behind where I am standing, but really no notice was taken of it, except a little knocking on the Speaker's desk, and a request on his part that members would resume their seats and keep order.

A VOICE:—Who where the members?

MR. CLINGMAN:—I do not give the names of the parties in any of these cases, because, if I did, I might have to refer to gentlemen who are now upon the floor, and thereby render it necessary for them to make explanations, and thus divert the attention of the House from the present case.

Sir, I recollect also that during the Congress of 1852, two gentlemen from Mississippi had a fight over the way; they were rather stout gentlemen, and made quite a "muss," as they say in New York, but nobody talked then of raising a committee. Why, even during the last Congress, I think we had two difficulties of this sort. A gentleman from Maine had a fight with some gentleman from the West, but it all ended without any action, or even notice, on the part of the House. On another occasion two gentlemen from Tennessee had a violent altercation, and one of them jumped over several desks, and the other pulled out a pistol, or, at any rate a pistol fell upon the floor near him; but no steps were taken against them. And it is a little remarkable that the gentleman who jumped over the desks was a candidate for an office in this House at the beginning of this session, and was elected on the first ballot by a very large vote. If you look at that vote, I expect you will find that every single gentleman who voted for the raising of this committee actually voted for him. Now, that shows you what was thought of assaults and batteries here on the floor. There is no doubt that this was an interruption of the business of the House—that it was a breach of privilege; and yet a large majority of the present House, including all those, I think, who sustain the action against Mr. Brooks, attached so little weight to it, that, when they had the whole United States to pick from, they selected that very gentleman to make a Clerk of the House of.

There have also been several duels, without anybody being punished for them. It is true that, when the Cilley duel occurred, owing to the fact that there was a great deal of political excitement at the time, and that it was supposed that Mr. Clay was connected with it, and some capital could be made against him and his party, the House did get up a committee, and had debates; but the matter was laid on the table, and instead, a very foolish law was passed on the subject of duelling. During the first Congress that I was here, a duel occurred between a member from Alabama and a member from North Carolina. A member from New York (Preston King) did then introduce a resolution; but, after a little debate, the House rejected it by laying it on the table. The last duel occurred in 1851, between a gentleman from Alabama and one from my own State, and the House took no notice of it at all.

Then, as to outside difficulties, such as this one which the gentleman from Ohio has now brought before us in the present case, we have had almost innumerable cases of them. During the Congress before the last, while the House was in session, and just by the door of the post-office, a member from New York beat the Postmaster-General, or some other member of the Cabinet, and nobody took any notice of it. Why, there was a man shot in the door of this hall some years ago, while there was a fight going on between two members in the House, but no one was punished for it. A friend besides me suggests that the House did raise a committee in that case. I believe it did; but that was all.

I might allude to many other circumstances of this kind. My object is to let the House see that this occurrence, as compared with similar ones, is sought to be greatly magnified.

www.ingramcontent.com/pod-product-compliance
Lightning Source LLC
Chambersburg PA
CBHW030016240426
43672CB00007B/967